Christianity in a Post-Atheist Age

Christianity in a Post-Atheist Age

Clive Marsh

scm press

. © Clive Marsh 2002

British Library Cataloguing in Publication data

A catalogue record for this book is available
from the British Library

0 334 02869 8

First published in 2002 by SCM Press
9–17 St Albans Place, London NI ONX

www.scm-canterburypress.co.uk

SCM Press is a division of
SCM-Canterbury Press Ltd

Typeset by Regent Typesetting
and printed in Great Britain by
Creative Print and Design, Wales

Contents

Introduction

In 1999, as thirty-somethings, Jane Craske and I wrote these words:

For those who . . . look beyond work . . . there are plenty of options. Leisure, health, sport, religion, shopping, entertainment: there is much of this in abundance. And this really is where religion comes in: it's a leisure pursuit which fights for a place (for those interested) in the middle of a crowded programme of televised sport, cinema, computer-games, shopping-expeditions, nights out, long-weekends, team-games and fitness drives. Or at least, the explicit 'collective worship' and 'meetings' aspects of religious practice fit in here. For that is where the time-pressure takes effect: there's always too much to do. In this context, if Christianity is to get much of a look-in, then it will have to demonstrate how the collective things are *worth* doing. And if these are worth doing, and are believed to be more than just isolated leisure pursuits, then a case will have to be made for how these collective activities (and whatever other individual activities should accompany the corporate pursuits) influence the rest of life. There's no escaping the fact, though, that at the moment, most of our contemporaries are shopping, visiting family and friends, sipping *café au lait* at the foot of the Eiffel Tower, donning a football shirt (to play or watch), or reading the newspaper on Sundays. They are not in church. And the truth is that even many of those who are in church feel a strong pull in other directions.[1]

I'm now over the hill, having turned forty. But this book is an attempt to address the challenge which Jane and I identified. My task is conceived less in terms of trying to persuade my contemporaries – of a similar age or younger – to 'go to church'. Rather, I want to argue the case for people being interested in and concerned about Christianity in British society today. Yes, this will entail

Why omit the definite article?

reference to, and complex entanglement with, 'church'. But I'd be on to a loser if I wrote a whole book about church. What I have to say undoubtedly has consequences for churches as we know them. But it is not my purpose to draw out those consequences fully here. I have no desire to try and save the Church. If the Church is worth saving, then this will come as a result of people appreciating much more besides: that it is worth believing something, that God is worth believing in, that Jesus Christ is worth following, that it is worth working at a practical 'spirituality' – that sort of thing.

The book is conceived as '95 discussion starters for bemused contemporaries'. The reasons for this are simple. In 1517, Martin Luther nailed '95 theses' to a German church door, criticizing the Church of his day. It was a key moment in the Protestant Reformation. Today, criticism of the Church doesn't have quite the same social, political or even religious effect. If Christianity is to be argued for, and its content re-worked and re-directed, then its audience must be different. The 'theses' will have to be different too. I am therefore offering ninety-five arguments in the form of discussion starters. Putting them on to paper has the advantage of giving about three months' worth of daily reading for those for whom theology books might usually be hard to stomach. And those who want to see all the ninety-five discussion starters before they even begin the book can see them all collected together as Appendix 1.

But who are the intended readers? In 1799, the German Protestant theologian Friedrich Schleiermacher published a set of *Speeches on Religion*. They had been written for the 'cultured despisers' of his day. There are plenty of despisers of Christianity, cultured and uncultured, around today. But the reconstruction and rediscovery of Christianity is more likely to come from elsewhere:

- from those who are hanging on in the church by their fingernails;
- from those who are sympathetic to what Christianity stands for, yet need some convincing that it really can bring itself into the modern and post-modern worlds;
- or from those who are far from convinced, but are far from cynical about religion, and are willing to listen.

Ian Hislop, editor of *Private Eye* and well-known British social commentator, has been quoted as saying: 'Sometimes I sit in church and think: "This is complete bollocks, all of it, and always has been," and then a month later I'd sit there thinking: "This is all there is."'[2] Such an attitude to Christianity sums up the terrifying ambiguity and perplexity of so many twenty-, thirty- and forty-somethings

And some of us can feel it in our position!

about religion today. This book simply tries to present a case for a kind of Christianity that retains some plausibility in the midst of this terrifying ambiguity.

The *first chapter* identifies the many aspects of human living which are touched upon by religious faith. I own up, as best as I can, to the prejudices I bring to my task in spelling out what readers will themselves need to put on the line in order to get the most from the book. The *second chapter* characterizes the context in which any set of arguments for the rediscovery or reassertion of Christianity has to be made. In particular I explore the question of whether we do indeed live in a 'secularized' society. In the *third chapter* I make clear the ways in which I am drawing on recent movements in theological thought. This is not just a 'background' chapter, as I already anticipate the emphases on which the whole tenor of my argument depends. Readers may be tempted to skip this chapter to begin with, and come back to it later. I hope you won't, for although you can move about between the discussion starters, there is a logical sequence in the way I present them. But I do accept that on a first read-through, this chapter may be tough.

The *fourth and fifth chapters* find me digging into my own tradition in search of forms of Christianity which seem especially worth re-shaping for today. Luther and Schleiermacher were both Protestants. There is no point my pretending that my use of these two Protestant giants is due simply to the form of their arguments at two key points in Western history. I am also drawing directly on Luther's and Schleiermacher's Protestantism, and on Schleiermacher's so-called liberalism. In Chapter 4 I offer a chastened form of Christian liberalism as the key to the style of new Christianity. Then, in Chapter 5, I examine what it might mean to draw contemporary resources for Christianity's future directly out of the history of Protestantism. Unlike much Protestantism, I am not interested in being anti-Catholic, merely in using the features of Protestantism which will actually work in the present. The *sixth chapter* is the practical climax of the argument, spelling out some of the main reasons why people should consider adopting a contemporary Christian faith and aspects of what that faith will need to be like. I continue to respect the fact that Christianity is one religion amongst many, whilst accepting that only a *particular* religious faith can be held. In an *Epilogue*, I spell out why it is important to consider the continuing potential of religious belief in Britain today.

I

Finding a Place to Start

One of the great gains of the contemporary world in which we live (often called 'post-modern') is that it has forced all writers to be as upfront as they can be about their own prejudices. The word 'prejudice', of course, is usually heard negatively. Yet we all have them: judgements we have already reached before we realize it, assumptions we have already made before we open our mouths. In a postmodern climate, we are forced to appreciate the extent to which there is no view 'from nowhere'. We are all situated, all conditioned, all limited, all perspectival in everything we say or do. This is both refreshing and frightening for any kind of religious faith. It's refreshing because it means that the specific forms of people's faith/s and religion/s get recognized. It's frightening because suddenly understandings of 'God' are up for grabs too. If you can never appear to deal with 'God' but only with people's perspectives on God, then we have reached the horror scenario that we can never be sure of dealing with anything else *but* people's faith. We can never be sure we deal with God – as reality – at all.

In the midst of this horror scenario there is the danger that we realize just how self-absorbed we all are, and how little objectivity there is. When we thought we might have been talking about God, the world, or reality, perhaps we really have been talking only about ourselves. Post-modernism has exposed the chimera of objectivity in all human knowledge, only to turn us into narcissists (who keep looking at themselves and worshipping what they see) or even solipsists (who don't believe that anything else exists except themselves).

This is a powerful challenge to any attempt to have a serious look at what religion has been up to and might yet achieve. But it is too pessimistic a picture. We don't have to conclude, when we realize that God-talk (theology) is difficult, that we are probably not speaking of God at all. We just have to be very careful with what we say, and with what we do on the basis of what we say. Because we see that we are directly implicated in what we say about God doesn't mean that we're speaking only about ourselves. But the close relationship between God-talk and human concerns does mean that we will only want to explore the contemporary possibilities for some kind of religious faith in close alliance with the issues which actually face us. We shall not simply be dealing with 'big questions', however true it may be that religion faces such questions head-on. We shall have to respect the mundane and the everyday. For if this book fails to offer a way of reading 'religion' in relation to 'everyday life', then it will not have served its purpose.

The book begins, then, with a series of discussion starters inviting readers to identify for themselves their own prejudices and starting-points. In order to issue the challenge I shall be unashamedly auto-biographical. I risk the charge of post-modern self-absorption. But it's a risk worth taking. For I want the book to engage with readers, and I want readers to open up to get the most from the book. The basic question coming out of Chapter 1 is this: who are you, and why should you bother with religion? The best way to use the discussion starters in this first chapter, then, is not simply to determine what you like or don't like about me (you'll do that anyway). I invite you to use the subject matter of each, prompted by the autobiographical paragraphs, to face up to the many dimensions of human life that we need to give thought to, and with which religion unavoidably deals. You could consider every discussion starter, then, ending with the question: 'And what about *you*?'

No religion or world-view can, or should, dodge questions of biology, embodiment and sexual identity.

I am male. I have been shaped by the many formative influences of Western culture 1960–2000 as they have evolved from fashioning the bread-winning male to the New Man. I did not choose pink clothes as a child, did not do sewing at school, got into sport in a big way, am competitive at games of all kinds, hardly spoke to anyone until my twenties about sexuality, and have found it a struggle to speak openly and creatively about emotions. However, I chose languages, not science, as main school subjects, have never been terribly robust physically, was never very good at sport (but enjoyed and still enjoy it immensely), am told that I am sensitive to people's feelings (and oversensitive with regard to my own) and do most of the cooking at home. Whether any of this makes me a New Man I'm not sure. I still wrestle with the extent to which my masculinity has been clearly culturally shaped. But I was given a body with male features, and am very comfortable with most of it. Those bits I am not too happy with don't cause me too much grief.

Most of my religious upbringing didn't encourage me to think too much about my body. Reflections on embodiment came later in life, in the wake of developments of thinking in both religion and society. I have been glad that this has happened, for this reflection fitted in well with my exploration of my own sexuality. Unlike a clergyman I once worked with who expressed indignance at the impact of feminism upon church life and stated 'it shouldn't be a major issue as to whether I take my penis to meetings', I have ended up concluding that the fact my penis is always with me affects who I am, all of the time. I don't think I am wholly controlled by my maleness. But I cannot avoid its profound impact upon who I am, and the inevitable limitations it brings with it (I am not female).

No religion or world-view can, or should, dodge questions of sexual orientation.

I am heterosexual. I'd be lying if I said I'd ever had any obvious homosexual urges. I haven't. Maybe I have and I've suppressed them. I certainly have close male friends. All I can say is that I'm not conscious of having been sexually attracted to them. But I accept that it may be because I've been conditioned by the traditional 1960s–70s world in which I grew up that I feel thoroughly heterosexual. At any rate, my sexual urges find their fullest physical expression in my relationship with my wife, the partner I have been with for sixteen years, and, I guess, in lots of other sublimated ways (sport and the arts especially).

None of this means I assume heterosexuality to be for everyone. It can be regarded as the norm only in the sense that most people in most cultures seem sexually attracted to the opposite sex. But there are clearly homosexual and bisexual people around who are comfortable with their sexual orientation.

For much of my adult life, however, the question of the acceptance of homosexual orientation and practice as equally acceptable to that of heterosexuals – morally, socially and within religion – has been one of the most pressing issues that the religion of which I have been a part (Christianity) has faced. It remains unresolved. And in acknowledging that 'some of my best friends are homosexual' I must also accept a struggle with my own homophobia.

Whether readers do or do not have any particular religious affiliation, this will have been an issue that has accompanied them throughout their adult life. It is very important, therefore, that readers try and tease out what they really think, and whether they are aware why they think as they do.

Our habits of consumption implicate us daily in a messy and complex world.

I am a consumer and do the main family grocery shopping. I sometimes like going to shopping malls when there are specific things which need to be bought. I even impulse buy occasionally. But I am alarmed at how cheaply we can sometimes buy things, knowing what this means for the people who grew or made what we buy in the West. I was a voluntary sales representative for a fair trade organization for seven years in the late 1980s and early 1990s. This experience taught me a lot and shaped some of my buying patterns. I am less scrupulous and thus more oppressive in my purchasing than I was. But at least the interwovenness of religion, world awareness and consciousness of living in a global market has contributed to the way I do some of my shopping.

At the time of writing (mid-2001) there is widespread concern about the major world summits which are meeting (in Seattle, Gothenberg and Genoa) to discuss matters of world trade. Even some of the major political lobbying groups (e.g., Friends of the Earth) have eventually had to withdraw from protest because of some of the violent forms which these protests have begun to take. But it is clear that issues which have been part of me because of my religion for many decades are well and truly alive in the international political arena. I have been enabled to see the link between the coffee that I drink and the profits that multinational companies make.

I am aware, too, both that the issues are more messy than they are often presented to me, and that the economic context in which all the discussions about trade happen has been changing around me. Capitalism appears to have won the economic war world-wide.[1] The challenge is how a caring capitalism might be possible (if, indeed, it is). But I have become more of a capitalist than I wanted to be through these major changes. I was a shareholder, for a time, of a major building society without wanting to be. In selling the shares, I received money I did not ask for. As a husband of a Methodist minister, I do not own a house, or have a mortgage. This means my wife and I must, as best we can, plan for retirement. The question 'to whom should we entrust any money we save?' is a burning issue. From a contemporary religious faith I would expect some guidance on all such issues. If a faith were not giving me some lead on how to spend and use money, then it would not be a relevant faith. I'll always need to make my own decisions, and do not expect to disengage my rational faculties at this point. But I think it reasonable to assume that the substance of one's religious faith should be entangled with such questions.

The fact that the membership of the churches is ageing and declining substantially does not mean that Christianity has nothing to offer the under-fifties.

I'm in my early forties. For all of my adult life I've been in ageing churches in numerical decline, though I often haven't realized it at the time. Indeed, at some points, I have been protected from the scale of this by the company I have kept. As a student in the late 1970s and early 1980s, it seemed as if Christianity was upbeat and that as Christians we really would change the world (alongside those of other religious traditions, and in partnership with well-meaning – if misguided – humanists). It was some time before I realized that people had been hoping for better things of Christianity since the early 1960s! Now, though, things are undoubtedly at crisis point. Some denominations may simply disappear in Britain in twenty to thirty years unless they refocus, expand their membership, or allow themselves to become small introverted groups concerned simply about their own survival. Re-focusing, re-invention *and* expansion of membership seem to be the best available options. This book is meant to contribute to that discussion.

I'd be deluding myself, though, if I were to suggest that religion – and in my own case, Christianity – had done nothing for me. I must accept that this whole project has a sense of 'look what it did for me' about it. However, this book is not an exercise in mere self-expression. Furthermore, for Christianity in the present and the future to do what it did for me back in the 1970s and 1980s, it will need in any case to function quite differently. In terms of the age of people it will be able to connect with, it will be important to recognize that churches do their work best precisely because they are unusual in bringing together in a locality people *of different ages*. Churches can easily look like 'families' (in a good sense) because of the way that people within them relate across generations. But at the same time as continuing to operate in this counter-cultural, life-enhancing way, the relatively small numbers of people under fifty who currently attach themselves to Christianity will undoubtedly need to think carefully about the nature and style of their involvement.[2] They will need to bunch up. People in their twenties, thirties and forties will need to meet to discuss the things that matter to them, and to compare notes. If they don't, a connected, vibrant faith will become disconnected and dead.

For a connected faith to be kept alive, people will continually need to be assured that it will be worth their while spending time on 'the religion thing'. There is a self-interest element at work here. But let's not pretend it hasn't always been so. 'Salvation' is a self-interested thing in so far as people would not be interested in it if salvation weren't available to them too. So we needn't worry about appealing to the benefit of religion to people in trying to commend it. Error only creeps in when we imply that religion can be 'sold' and 'bought' like a commodity and that it requires nothing very demanding of those who get into it. There is evidence that people are being turned off mainstream religion just now precisely because it is not demanding enough, and is of too little help in enabling people to live their lives. Precisely because religion inevitably gets tangled up in the highs and lows of life, and in the deepest questions which life presents, it will (should!) prove a stretching exercise. It is, then, time to find a new way of offering a religious faith and life to people who haven't yet been asked enough to try one out.

Where you've lived is who you are.

I have lived in South Yorkshire for ten years. Before that I've lived on Merseyside, in Bangor (North Wales), in Oxford and in East London. Interspersed within that were a year in South Germany, and three months in Chicago. Apart from holidays, I have spent little time living 'in the country'. I have had only one year living outside of an urban or inner-city setting (and that was in Germany). I have no experience of living in the Southern Hemisphere. I am writing this in the USA during my first experience of 'small town American life' (a Summer in South Carolina).

All of these places have left deep impressions on me and have contributed to the shaping both of who I am and the particular version of the Christian faith I carry with me. I was born in Liverpool, and Liverpool remains my home city. I have a romantic, nostalgic, tribal attachment to it which is irrational. I grew up eight miles away from the city, and had school friends who, when they went away to university or to work beyond the region, were embarrassed about their origins. They said they were from St Helens, lest people assume that they were going to have their wallet pinched. I chose not to disown my roots, though I understand why my friends behaved in this way. It took me some years to realize it, but I suspect that a lack of confidence I still possess in polite company might go back to these experiences.

Seven years' higher education inevitably changed me. But the geography is as significant as the time in the lecture and seminar-room. To take the obvious example: I enjoyed Oxford immensely, but was in many ways like a fish out of water. I lived most of the time in East Oxford (near Cowley), and, on reflection, had relatively little to do with formal university life. I read in its libraries, ate its dinners, played sport on its playing fields, and some of its students remain close friends. But being a student was like 'doing a job' which happened to be in that city. I went as a graduate, and therefore essentially went to write a book over a three-year period. The more significant aspect of my life there was my involvement in (Methodist) church life. It is, however, striking what assumptions people make about you throughout British society – in the academy too – when you're known to have had 'an Oxford education'.

The way in which my Christian faith had been shaped from the start, however, means that it has always been inextricably enmeshed with where I have lived. However timeless and detached 'the faith' may have been presented to me as being, it is clear that somehow I was enabled to see that if the faith I professed was not profoundly rooted – concretely – in where I lived, then it was no real, Christian faith.

Geography does not, of course, only affect our religious beliefs. It affects our political commitments and perhaps our health and wealth too. But whether or not we are religious may well be because of where we've been. As an Irish student I once knew said when he discovered I studied theology: 'I'm from Ireland. I've had it up to here with religion.'

Ethnicity matters. *A dear We start th Smith Christian!*

I'm a WASP (White, Anglo-Saxon Protestant). I wasn't aware of my whiteness until I began to meet black people. I'm not sure I'd heard the word 'racist' until I'd left the Liverpool area, though that wouldn't be true now. It was some years before I began to appreciate how racist I was, and thus no doubt remain. But many life experiences have caught me short in this area: in multi-cultural churches in East London and in the South Side of Chicago especially. The limitations of one's ethnic and national backgrounds, however, and of the profound necessity to explore them, are now very apparent to me. The last ten years or so in Europe have shown again just how important the interweaving of religion with ethnic and national identity is.

British society struggles to release itself from the fact that because most of its recent history has been 'Christian' its primary purpose is to recover a sense of 'Christendom', or to bemoan Christendom's loss. Wrapped up with this is the mistaken assumption that Christendom must be white. But the domination of both must be seen as having come to an end. Britain has many ethnic cultures and many religions. Ethnicity and religious belief interweave, but are far from identical. And people do change religions. But ethnicity matters. And it is white people who need to begin to appreciate this more than most.

Who says it?

Religious particularity matters. Denominations may be less important than they were, but respect for them is necessary. Otherwise, we're too general and universal for our own good.

I am a Methodist. Having been brought up in a Christian Brethren family, I spent time amongst Anglicans in Wales, Lutherans in Germany, and then Methodists in Oxford. I learned much from each of those movements as I continue to do so, but it is with Methodists that I happen to have remained. For much of my adult life, though, there has been a sensitivity about stressing denominational distinctives because of the damage such emphasis might do to the ecumenical cause. Recently, however, ecumenism (after a postwar high) has struggled. Much ecumenism has been brought about by local numerical or economic necessity rather than theological insight or genuine goodwill. And it's been clear for some time now that there are drawbacks when ecumenism leads to rootlessness. All Christians will need to plant roots somewhere, and will be depending on spiritual and theological roots which are tangled up with some denomination or other, at some point.

Not always DARNALL ?

There has been an appropriate backlash against 'common denominator ecumenism', that style of co-operation between churches which seems so anxious about offending that it means people do and say very little. Any recovery of the sense of Christianity's usefulness in the future, though, will need to be explicit about what roots are being tapped. There will not be only one form of such tapping. Reformed Christians, Roman Catholics, Evangelical Anglicans, Baptists, Anglo-Catholic Anglicans, Methodists, Charismatic Pentecostalists (to name but a small range of the available options) will all be able to offer different versions of the roots that are needed. But such a short list is evidence that there are religious resources 'out there' which can help people shape a framework within which to live their lives.

Family histories interweave with the development of our beliefs and values to a profound extent, and are often insufficiently examined.

I am the dutiful son of God-fearing parents (father and mother an electrician and milliner respectively), brother to a printer and graphic-designer whose faith still has meaning for him, and grandson of two working-class Christian families. One grandfather was a retailer of household goods and electrical supplies, the second was a merchant seaman. Only recently have I learned that my sea-faring grandfather was lost at sea for many months during World War II. Even now I have scarcely begun to appreciate the impact of my grandfather often being away for many months upon my grandmother and mother. I have, though, sought to make sense of some of my family's war experiences – in particular my mother's unhappy evacuation to Cheshire from bombed-out Liverpool (she returned to the city despite the bombing, with grave consequences to her health).

These are the very normal stories of most English families during the period 1930–2000. The detail could be extended. Were I to ask for similar stories of those amongst whom I now live, the accounts would take in the steel industry, mining, long hours, industrial accidents, work-related illnesses, social stability, extended families. Such detail, though, is crucial to accounts of how beliefs and values get shaped and the form and content of any resulting faith. It is easier to hold to a belief in an all-powerful, caring God when a seaman safely returns. In my grandmother's case, I have little doubt that her faith would have remained firm had my grandfather not returned. She struggled enough in life as it was. But in contemporary, relatively prosperous Britain such a faith is clearly less easy to come by, let alone sustain. I am, however, affected by having seen faith in practice at first hand through family members.

Religious belief and practice, or the lack of both, cannot but be interwoven with such family experiences. It is still the case that most people in Britain have had some contact with religion within their family life. Such contact may take a variety of forms, and be positive, negative or, more likely, a mixture of the two. Some experience over-exposure to religion through compulsory attendance at religious occasions via school, or at religious schools. Others have had contact with Sunday schools or keep in touch via 'rites of passage' (baptisms, weddings and funerals). It remains unusual for religion – which for most Britons still, largely, means Christianity – to have played no part at all in family histories. Things are changing, admittedly. In some parts of British society, it has now got to the stage where parents are feeling compelled to become interested in Christianity through their children. Children are wanting to know why their parents either have no religion, or seem to want to protect their children from it.

of Callum Brown.

We are, then, not just where we've been, but also who we've been with. This means that the relations or the 'family-like' friends that we've lived with, or spent a lot of time with, have played a huge part in shaping who we are, and the beliefs and values we have. If we have any explicitly religious beliefs, then these will have derived from, or been reactions to, the beliefs and values of those close to us. It's a simple point. I remain amazed at how little people often explore this facet of contemporary living.

Parenthood can be preoccupying.

The question of 'family', though, also takes us in other directions. I am now a father. I have regularly been bored by preachers who draw so many of their life illustrations from 'family life'. Children do indeed provide us with powerful images, both in what they themselves ask or say, and in the degree to which they extend our knowledge of ourselves and the world around us. But parents can become tiresome when they begin to articulate their faith at all points solely in relation to the experience of parenthood. Admittedly, parenthood becomes all-consuming. There is no let-up to being a parent. As a parent it quickly becomes clear how and why questions of God as 'father' (or mother, or parent) interlock so fundamentally with basic concerns about human identity.

But this is slippery territory too. Talk of 'family values' is too easy. It's as if we know what family values are without too much exploration. And though all have parents (even if some do not know precisely who their parents are), not all are parents themselves. The 'family' encompasses neither in theory nor practice all that human experience and religions have to handle in the realm of personal relationships. The interplay of religious and family life is thus a minefield. It is a crucial area in need of exploration, and a danger zone.

Having said all this, parenthood is a profound experience, the significance of which cannot be downplayed in its impact not only on self-understanding and ethical conduct, but also upon the shaping of religious convictions.

Meaningful activity (work) is crucial in human life, but is not everything.

My wife and I have sought, throughout our married life, to alternate as to which of us is the primary 'bread-winner'. Since having children, we have both been in full-time employment for just three months, and concluded that, for all four of us, this was not a wise move (it was hell). We are conscious that to have the economic stability and freedom to be able to do this is something not possible for all. We are, though, scarcely wealthy. It is a choice we have made, even though our combined income is not very far above average in Britain (and is considerably lower than that enjoyed in North America).

But we'd be deluding ourselves if we weren't aware of how much structured work provides for us as individuals well beyond the material rewards: a sense of worth, a chance to exercise abilities and skills discovered and worked on earlier in life, the opportunity to make use of qualifications gained, a pattern in life, and healthy time away from each other and our children. But work has its limits too. For many (especially the middle classes across the Western world), the question of balancing work, family and leisure becomes the subject of many a newspaper and magazine article, and a crucial discussion topic in the shared life of partners. For those without the leisure time or economic freedom even to consider the question realistically (or a partner to share the load), the issues that the question raises are no less pressing.

For me personally, switching in and out of full-time work, and taking on a major role in childcare, have together been amongst the most instructive challenges in life. They have contributed hugely to helping me grasp what life might be about, and how religious practice and belief help to make sense of it. The juggling act has forced upon me, and never in isolation from others, radical questions of prioritizing. Without religion as part of the mix, and without supposing that religion simply delivers easy solutions to the choices that have to be made, I am not clear I would have been pressed so hard as to the value system, or systems, within which solutions are reached.

The psychological aspects of the question of 'class and Christianity' in Britain have been inadequately explored.

My roots are working-class, and I'd have been regarded as brought up amongst the 'urban poor'. For the first eighteen years of my life I lived in an area later classified as an Urban Priority Area. For the first ten of those years I lived in a house with no bathroom. I discovered later that for someone of my age this was quite unusual. (It gave me more in common with those much older than I.) As a young teenager I accompanied my father, and occasionally worked, on building sites. The economic stability of family life was subject to jobs being secured by my self-employed father, and then on people actually paying their bills. We 'never went without' (the goal of any self-respecting working-class family) but I only recently discovered how low the family finances sometimes were. I am grateful that these days did not coincide with the 'credit boom', although I doubt that my family would ever have chosen to take advantage of such a boom even so.

Alongside, and often in conflict, with these realities, though, was the prosperity theology (God will provide not only what you need, but a lot more) implied in much of the preaching and biblical exposition I heard throughout my youth. I can now see the existence of some basic creative tensions: in economic experience (between relative hardship and the evident material wealth of some well-known visiting preachers), and in the task of interpreting the Christian tradition (between the seemingly clear-cut interpretations being implied, and the things I was noting in the Bible open in front of me which seemed to contradict what many preachers said). Most of my own Christian life and subsequent academic theological endeavour have been about the exploration of those tensions.

Of course, there is a clear sense in which I am no longer 'working-class'. I 'got education'. I 'got out' and 'made it good'. I have become middle-class by virtue of educational qualifications, 'professional standing' and disposable wealth. But things aren't, I think, quite that simple. I quickly saw that without the system of grants operating in the late 1970s in Britain, I'd probably never have gone into Higher Education.[3] Other people's past political decisions, for which I remain profoundly grateful, enabled my 'getting out and getting on'. I have met many such people, now in powerful positions in Higher Education and elsewhere, who have come through a similar route and would be intrigued to see a socio-psychological study undertaken of such 'working-class people' in such positions. My hunch is that we are all still wrestling with the tensions of working-class origins in our jobs, and struggling with mindsets and structures which jar at many points.[4]

I also wrestle with the tension between the seeming need to undergo a geographic shift – to be displaced – in order better to understand where I was from, and who I had become, and yet the deep loyalty I still feel to where I grew up. I did not consciously leave my home because of dislike of either home or locality, or in any quest to change my social status. I am not even sure I wanted to 'get on in the world'. I simply wanted to learn, and get some sort of interesting job, and needed to take advice on how to do that. This meant leaving home and studying more. But the geographical shift has undoubtedly been enriching, whilst causing socio-psychological complications in class terms. In terms of religion, the 'class thing' remains a live issue. I do not expect to have power. I assume that someone somewhere else will make, and will have made, decisions over which I have no control. The 'truth is' that this is only partially the case. I now have power of all kinds, and enjoy having it.

It is, though, logical that I have stumbled into Methodism, not the denomination of my youth. Methodism embodies as a movement precisely the class struggle I have experienced in my own life. It is a largely middle-class church which pretends not to be (and in a few significant respects *is* not). It is a movement with a clear legacy of contact with, and membership of, working-class people. Scratch the surface of some of its current leaders and you'll find a working-class kid beneath. But as to the extent to which Methodism fully developed, or has maintained, its ability to be a British Christian movement for 'ordinary people', that is another matter. It remains now as a challenge for contemporary Methodism to redefine and refocus its mission.

'Class and Christianity' in Britain needs further study. Many fine historical studies of class, and of aspects of Church history's entanglement with questions of class, exist. But the area of enquiry needs further and deeper treatment with regard to theology and spirituality. What different kinds of Christians result from out of the complex, but persistent, British class structure? What is to be done with the fact that people often assume that churchgoing is to do with social aspiration? What of the fact that involvement in Christianity can actually lead to people having personal habits which mean they end up better off (e.g., because, for whatever reason, they change what they spend their money on, and have more disposable income)? All such practical questions are contained within the tensions which class-consciousness and Christianity open up.

All religion is political.

I am a member of the British Labour Party. I was brought up in a working-class Tory household. With hindsight, some things are very clear. There was an easy alliance between the individualist piety of the evangelicalism in which I grew up, my father's self-employed status, Labour's ascendancy in the period of strong trade unions (I lived in the constituency of Harold Wilson, including during his time as Prime Minister) and support for the Conservative Party. The religious belief-system I was presented with was (ostensibly) profoundly apolitical. Of course, it was nothing of the sort. I was in my twenties before I began to appreciate all of this. My 'political conversion' was not, however, sudden, and even now I feel quite sure that Old Labour supporters would doubt the sincerity of it, especially as I joined the SDP for a time. Even so, evangelicalism and Tory origins are a powerful combination of factors militating against a wholesale conversion to socialism.

But what has happened is that I have shifted from the political quietism espoused by my upbringing, and seen (both through theology and politics) the importance of the social, of community, and of corporateness in human living. I am less individualist, without having lost sight of the crucial significance of the individual in any social context. But I am also very clear that there is no apolitical religion, and no non-political religious faith. Furthermore, any Christian who declares that 'you can be political without being party political' in any unqualified sense, is simply misguided.

* * *

I have used my own autobiography to demonstrate how my religious journey has interwoven with some of the main questions that all of us have to face as human beings. The main point of this first chapter, though, has been to require you, the reader, to do some work about your own origins, background and life history so that you are well-prepared for the arguments that follow in later chapters. If you're to get most from this book, then you'll have to put where you've come from, are now, and think you're heading, on the line. Only in this way will you genuinely be able to ask the question how and where Christianity (or religion, in whatever forms) has interwoven with your life experience, and/or where it might yet connect.

I have been autobiographical both to make this first part compelling, but also to make it concrete. We cannot speak of Christian faith in the abstract. Like any religion, Christianity always has to take concrete shape. One of the questions left for readers, then, is what kinds of Christianity, if any, you have encountered, and whether those encounters were positive or negative. I am also assuming that readers will have begun to ask themselves broader questions than whether they are, or have been, explicitly 'religious'. Religious faith takes shape within, and in relation to, 'real life', not as a 'parallel universe'. It has therefore been important for all readers to become clear about the many aspects of their lives with which Christian faith can and should interweave.

2

Still Spiritual after All These Years:
The Religious Context

Having raised questions about the kinds of issues – life issues – with which religion interweaves, it is now time to consider the context within which the question of religion's contemporary viability has to be posed. If bemused onlookers are to be encouraged to give a religious way of living more serious consideration, then they have to be enabled to clarify the features of contemporary society into which such a religious outlook might fit. If the residually religious are to be challenged to make their religion live a bit more, then they too need to see what the point of such a religious revival would be. I speak here, of course, primarily out of a British context. The discussion starters offered, however, do take some account of Britain's location within a wider context.

Not every aspect of social and cultural change is, of course, dealt with in this chapter. The changing position and status of religion and the religions happens in a context where many major institutions are themselves undergoing great change: the monarchy, the armed forces, the legal profession, the medical profession, school education, higher education, not to mention the structure of the British government itself. Other facets of major change – e.g., increased ethnic diversity, religious pluralism, increased material prosperity for the many – are relevant too, and are touched on in different ways in other chapters. My purpose in this chapter is not to offer an exhaustive and comprehensive account of such change, but rather to paint a picture in broad strokes of what's been happening to Christianity within the widest possible understanding of the cultural framework of Britain in its place in Western society.

Western society has undoubtedly become more 'secular' over the past couple of centuries.

The decline of Christianity in Britain, and in the West generally, is easy to state, and relatively easy to log. Fewer people are church-goers than was the case in the nineteenth century. Fewer are, in practical terms, influenced on a daily basis by an explicit theology, or by a religious outlook on life. God may well be believed in only slightly less throughout the western world (though even this is statistically disputable), but God does not seem to make much practical difference to people. This process of 'secularization' is evident not only in personal terms. It can be argued for also in terms of the apparently declining social and political clout of religion, and of Christianity especially, throughout the western world. Governments no longer expect to have to pay as much attention to churches as they do their work.[1]

All of this amounts to the so-called 'secularization thesis'. Formulated and propounded by sociologists from the 1960s into the 1990s and to the present day, the secularization thesis attempts both to describe and to account for the waning impact of religion (especially Christianity) on western societies and individuals. As a thesis, it is still widely held in a variety of different forms, even if not by the majority of the leading sociologists of religion.[2] It is alive and well in much common discussion about religion (in and out of the press). It thrives even in churches, where the numerical decline of membership implies that 'religiosity' of all kinds must largely have come to an end, because 'the young don't come any more'. However, as a thesis, it is also widely disputed, first and foremost by sociologists of religion. Something has undoubtedly happened in western society, which has been summed up by the term 'secularization'. But whether this term quite captures what has happened is a different matter. There has been numerical decline in explicit membership of, and attachment to, organized religion throughout the West. There has been a challenge to Christianity's authority in ethical matters. But whether 'secularization' describes adequately the way that whilst organized religion's role appears to have decreased, religiosity has not disappeared, is a moot point.

Sociologists still in favour of the thesis can cede some ground here. What has been brought about is the *privatization* of religion. Religion has become so preoccupied with matters of personal (i.e., individual) taste and choice, that it no longer really matters what one believes. 'Secularization' is thus the *de facto* lack of impact of any communally held belief system in the public realm.

Understood in this way, it is difficult to argue against the existence of secularization in some form. But as the thesis takes practical shape, and in the form in which it is often presented, it holds little water. The deeper question is to account for what has happened to what we may call the dispersion of religion in the West into a variety of other forms of human practice. If religiosity does not disappear, but simply mutates, then the substitutes for religion (sport, shopping, sexual activity), the new religions (e.g., New Religious Movements) and the wide interest in spirituality need to be considered in terms of their social and political impact. It is not enough to say that religion has been privatized. Socially and politically committed forms of Christianity have existed throughout the period studied by the sociologists. It remains to be shown how and why particular forms of Christianity have been more prominent than others throughout the most recent period of Christianity's history in the West, and what new forms may yet emerge. The undoubted accuracy of a limited form of the 'secularization thesis' thus needs qualification at a number of points.

There are different kinds of western 'secularization'.

Even at its simplest, the secularization thesis can be shown to over-simplify a range of different ways in which the declining social and political impact of religious practice and belief takes shape. Easy reference to the role of 'religion in the West' begs questions. Which religion? Which western country? Even narrowing the discussion down to Christianity's cultural influence invites reflection on the version of Christianity being referred to. To take the most obvious example of a contrast in understandings of secularization in western culture, the difference in relations between Christianity and the state between Britain and the USA leads to differing readings of the secularization process. Thus, a federal system such as the USA which built into its constitution a separation of church from state has produced a form of secularization in which it proves difficult to make religious belief have a direct, formal impact in the ethical and political decisions which have to be taken. In this sense it is one of the most secularized countries on earth. *ask Bush!*

But, of course, social and political life in America is steeped in religion. Religion and politics simply relate differently there than they do in Britain. The somewhat archaic British example of the close alliance of religion and politics – the establishment of the Church of England – is but a different understanding of how to fashion the ethical significance of Christianity. In Britain, it is still assumed to be important that a formal link should be maintained between forms of government and mainstream religion. The form of this link will surely change at some point in the near future. But it is likely that it will be maintained in some form.

We can now see that the Pilgrim Mothers and Fathers who landed in Cape Cod on 9 November 1620 were escaping an enforced form of ecclesiastical life, not the principle of working out a theologically metaphysical approach to human living. It is thus not the different political structures themselves which account for secularization. But they do account for the different forms of secularization which result. *This is much more complex than Marx seems to realise*

Britain is less secular than often appears.

Somewhat perversely, the persistence of establishment in Britain, despite its archaic quality and the existence of many opponents (not least within the Church of England itself), is a sign that all is not lost for religion, and even for Christianity, in Britain today. There are, though, many other signs too. I need simply to list them here before going on to use the evidence collected in other points below. Folk/common/implicit religion abounds still. It was present in peculiar, not yet fully understood, form at the time of the death of Diana, Princess of Wales, in 1997. It is evident every Summer in the well dressing ceremonies which take place in parts of rural England. It surrounds baptismal and funeral practices, when time-honoured family traditions, sometimes little understood and rarely reflected upon, are repeated. *I blame the WELLS at Nkewill :– 1956!!*

And then there is the spirituality boom. You only need visit one of the main chain bookstores in Britain, take a close look at airport bookstalls, or pay attention to what's being sold in garden centres and supermarkets ('mood music' CDs and collections of wise sayings above all), to realize that spiritualities of all kinds are being actively promoted just now. Critics may be being too cynical if they suggest that this is merely to do with profit seeking. Understanding 'the market' is admittedly not a simple task in any sphere of life. But record companies and publishers don't usually bother promoting such movements in economically unviable settings. Whatever else it may be achieving, the spirituality boom exists because it meets a consumer demand. It is worth asking why there is the demand.

There are also substitutes for religion. Sport (participatory and spectator), shopping (spending, and mall-visiting), travel (e.g., Disneyworld as a place of pilgrimage) and the arts (galleries, film-watching and film-going, poetry, music-playing, concert-going, literary groups) are especially prominent. Some of these practices interweave with religion as more commonly understood, of course (the arts especially). Some may be seen to have replaced religion to such an extent that it may appear religion has reached the point of no return. A more plausible reading of what's going on, however, is that many such practices have reached a fresh intensity in the face of the decline of traditional religious practices. Support for football teams, therefore, meets a social, psychological and even pseudo-metaphysical need in people in so far as it provides a life-shaping framework for living. Football support shapes the year, and the week (between August and May). It provides a liturgy. It gives meaning. It provides a community. Viewing the practice of football support in this way may not simply be a matter of drawing a comparison, but of religious practice and sporting support mutually critiquing each other. There may be a new understanding of religion in contemporary society yet to emerge as a result of this. Religious believers may want to keep on saying that football support really will never be sufficient for a fully lived life. Football supporters may already be at the point of showing just how far mainstream religions have moved from what they are meant to be and do.

There are, then, many ways in which the religiosity of British society should not be underplayed.

British people are often more secular than they realize.

However, even having granted a pervasive, lingering religiosity, and new or substitute forms of religion, the converse of the claim that 'there's more religion around than we realize' is also true. Even where religion explicitly surfaces it is often in highly secular forms. Lingering religiosity keeps at arm's length any form of demanding religion (i.e., a religion which actually requires a fair degree of commitment from its practitioners). Individualistic spiritualities – those which seem to address the needs of the individual consumer – frequently don't demand that people face up to the messiness and complexity of having to create communities with others (some of whom may be difficult, or at least very, very different). At their best religions require of people that they deal with what it means to create bodies of people (across cultures, ethnicities, ages, sexes and sexual orientations) who see themselves as bound together as equals before God. There is no dodging this. Any religious belief or practice which fails to require of its practitioners that they address such a central question, and fashion their lives accordingly, may well serve individual interests. But in not relating to the whole of a religious practitioner's life, it can be nothing but a disappointing form of religion.

But it is not only those who seem on or beyond the fringes of mainstream religion that can be critically examined at this point. The stalwart faithful in Christianity, too, should have awkward questions posed of them. Despite the professed commitment of many Christian people, the question 'What does your religion actually amount to?' can pointedly be asked of too many of us. Only slightly in jest have I led an adult education session in Christian circles around the thesis: 'The widespread practice of caravanning was the single major cause of the decline of Christianity in Britain in the second half of the twentieth century.' This example can be multiplied. There are simply too many things which religious believers allow to distract them from their religion.

Now this area of exploration admittedly needs some caution. Caravanning at the weekend may actually be a very wholesome thing to do. If it enables families to spend quality time together in the way that's not possible during the week, then it can be a good thing. If it enables overworking people to relax, then it must be beneficial. Understood in this way, it is easily compatible with some of Christianity's own concerns: the quality of human relationships and the need for a Sabbath. There is sometimes the danger that Christians see something as inimical to their religion if it simply disrupts the time-honoured structure of Sunday worship (and those of other religious traditions have their equivalents). It need not, of course, be so. But caravanning is a symbol of a whole range of activities and pursuits which may indeed be inimical to religious belief and practice.

In so far as caravanning (or weekend holidaying, city breaks, or their equivalent) distances people from their basic context of living or working, creates only temporary communities, serves only the interests of their participants, and fails to be related to any world-view or value-system within which people may choose to live their lives, then it is not conducive to religious interpretation. Religion is viewed as escapism by its critics. Too many of the distractions or disruptions to the possibility of religious practice are, however, also mechanisms of escapism from the challenges of contemporary human living. In this sense, despite the residual religiosity which can indeed be detected in British culture, people are often more secular than they realize.

World-views and value-systems are rarely recognized and shared.

As a corollary to the insight that British people are often more secular than they realize, we must note that the world-views and value-systems by which people live are insufficiently acknowledged. There are too few contexts in which people are pressed to identify the principles according to which they behave, and the ideologies or structures within which they believe. The residual Christianity still means that people in Britain are more likely to declare their religion to be 'Christian' if they declare anything at all (though many now profess no religious beliefs or affiliations). But in the absence of affiliation to a concrete set of believers (a church), this will never be pressed very far. Votes are cast every so often, inviting people to declare a political allegiance. But not everyone chooses to exercise their vote. And at least one main party has, somewhat bizarrely, spoken in recent years of trying to take ideology out of politics!

In such a philosophical climate it is easy to see how religion and theology might fare badly. Any system of thought, or set of principles or practices, is likely to struggle when ideology seems to matter little, and when people are required little to declare what they believe in. This will be especially true of a set of principles and practices which claims to speak of things which matter ultimately. As to the possibility of people sharing what they believe in, and the values that they live by, the old saying remains true: keep off all discussion about sex, death, religion and politics in British society, and you'll be fine.

British culture suffers from a legacy of bad religion.

Bad forms of Christianity from the past, however, may have contributed much to this state of affairs. There may well be residual Christianity, but for many that Christianity is an unhappy memory. It is the memory of being made to go to church, of 'enforced' or 'assumed' belief. It is the memory of stifling educational practices and 'heavy shepherding', in which there seemed little room to breathe or explore one's emerging beliefs and assumptions. For those who long since left behind explicit Christianity (as expressed in the practice of regular church-going), Christianity is now recalled as something unpleasant which happened to them as children. For some, like abusers who then abuse, it is even repeated in the form that 'my children should go through what I went through, it'll be good for them'. But parents are often not accompanying their children in their church-going. What then happens, is that Christianity remains a 'children's affair'. It is something which, like its non-participating adult adherents, never has the chance to be both grown-up and religious at the same time. There are, in short, good and bad aspects to the legacy of the Sunday school tradition.

Those who have had bad experience of Christianity and choose not to send their children to church escape from the religion inflicted upon them only to ignore the significance of religion altogether. But their Christianity frequently remains childish, as any cleric who visits parents who choose to re-connect with Christianity when offering children for baptism can testify. Remarkable as it may seem, the 'real existence' of Adam and Eve remains a stumbling block for many people in their thirties who last heard the story as seven-year-olds, believed it to be 'history as it really happened', and have since assumed that it must be thus believed as history by all Christians. Multiply such examples, and the sorry state of general education about Christianity and, by extension, religion's viability in Britain today becomes very apparent.

However, a legacy of bad religion does not mean that religion has no future. It merely sets an agenda for educational and religious institutions alike. It is into such a context that this present book must speak as it seeks to present a case not simply for the viability of religion in contemporary Britain, but also for the advisability of more people giving religion a serious look.

We live in a 'post-atheist' age.

How, then, is the current cultural mood to be characterized? It is post-modern, certainly, in the sense that the bravado of the Enlightenment, and its consequences in individualistic, progressive optimism (often summed up in the term 'modernism'), has been found wanting. But the Enlightenment neither derived from atheism, nor did it spawn atheism in any simple way. There is much over-simple referencing to the Enlightenment, especially amongst Christian theologians. Christianity and other forms of religion (especially deism) are admittedly keenly wrapped up in the Enlightenment and its aspirations. But like most revolutions, the Enlightenment is a complex phenomenon. Atheism is only part of its legacy. It is neither a greater nor lesser child of it than is individualistic, liberal Christianity (which can also claim other, deeper roots in Christianity and western culture).

If 'modernism' is being reacted against in our current age, it is not religion *per se* that is the main target. For those already predisposed to object to religion then it will be part of the modernist package which must be opposed. The post-modern climate is, however, being seen equally as an age within which religion (or, at least, religiosity or spirituality) might again find a place. At a time when the reach of an all-consuming technocratic rationality is questioned, religion can again find its place amongst the channels through which mystery, humanness, limitation, and awe re-assert themselves.

It is more appropriate, therefore, to speak of our age as 'post-atheist' rather than 'post-theist'. We may, admittedly, be less sure of God than we once were. We are certainly less clear who, and which movements or institutions, to turn to, to give us a lead as to what God might be like. But in our uncertainty, those of us who do believe in a religious kind of way appear more prone to believe any-thing rather than nothing. 'Post-atheism' in a time of weak religion is thus something of a frightening time. In the midst of considerable cultural disinterest in religion, there is nevertheless a lot of it about: religiosity is there for the taking. But the mainstream, more established religions don't appear to know quite what to do. At a time when all religions which have proved their worth – when offering their best – over many centuries could be setting about that task of clarifying how and why they have not only survived but been life-enhancing, Christianity appears as something of a dinosaur, and its churches as ageing, creaking institutions committed to preserving the dinosaur's memory.

Spirituality and religion are not the same thing.

We need, however, to note an important, basic distinction at this point. Spirituality and religion are not the same thing. Religion contains spirituality within it. (Or if it doesn't then it won't live.) Spirituality denotes the dynamic inner life which both drives a religious movement, and stimulates its individual members. Religion, though, is a set of principles and practices. In the present climate, it is clear that many people who are 'into religion' are really meaning that they are into spirituality. Some even speak in such terms. ('He's a deeply spiritual person, though he's not religious.' 'I have a spirituality, but I don't go to church or anything.')

Such a distinction correlates well with the concern that religion is being escaped from, or avoided. 'Religion' really can bind people with its demands. It can control people through the way in which it shapes their worlds. But unlike spirituality, which can sometimes imply that it is possible to be spiritual without being embodied, or without living in a concrete setting, and without really having much to do with the ordinary, messy things in life, religion is committed to respecting all such dimensions of life. It should, therefore, be the case that spirituality is indeed welcomed and encouraged, but that this happens within a lively religion.

There is a 'spirituality boom' happening at present, to which there are both positive and negative aspects.

The fact is, however, that religion is largely a 'no' word to great numbers of under-fifties in British culture, even if 'spirituality' may be acceptable to some. There is, though, as we noted earlier, something of a spirituality boom in Britain just now. What is to be made of this?

It is surely a good thing. It keeps alive a whole dimension of life which is in danger of being crushed in a technocratic, rationality-controlled age. In nurturing a sense of awe, mystery, human limitation, and, at its best, a concern for the other (other people, other cultures and worlds, other creatures, the natural world, the unknown other), the spirituality boom thus provides space within which religion can be seen still to have a role to play in western societies. It provides channels through which people who don't profess to be religious, and who would not darken the doors of synagogue, church, temple or mosque, can nevertheless get in touch with the kinds of things with which religions have always dealt.

But the spirituality boom also has its downside. Because of its frequent detachment from religions long tried and tested (and I am referring here not only to Christianity), some of the forms of spirituality which have appeared are insufficiently rooted in real life. Because of the implication that you can simply choose the bits of religiosity which you like best (hence, there is talk of 'pick-and-mix spirituality'), the spirituality boom goes hand in hand with a sense that it is a matter of indifference as to which spirituality you choose. The spirituality boom thus feeds individualism in religion.

What is more, the degree of detachment from mainstream religions (even though many ideas and beliefs held by contemporary spiritual people derive from mainstream religion) leads to the assumption that some of life's messiness can be side-stepped. If it's only possible to be religious (or spiritual) by avoiding the complexities of real religious communities, then this becomes simply another form of escapism. And at root, such an approach to religion may rest on a suspect view of what it means to be human, which mainstream theological anthropologies would be able to modify.

Mainstream religions need to re-assert themselves.

In such a context, it is time for mainstream religions to re-assert themselves. This will need to be done with great care. They will not be able simply to say that every need that the emergent spiritualities and the New Religious Movements are meeting will already easily be met in older, more established religions. It may be true. But those religions will need to work hard to prove that it is true. In all likelihood they will need to adjust and re-model themselves to show this. However, religions have not always proved themselves capable of appropriate change, or their organizations the most adaptable when needing to cope with social, cultural and political change.

What is more, given the regular opposition to religion *per se* in the pages of many newspapers and throughout popular culture, there is an apologetic task for religion itself which will need to be undertaken. Letters to newspapers along the lines of 'what has religion ever done for us? . . . produced wars etc. . . . you don't have to be religious to be moral . . .' appear at regular intervals in the broadsheets, and represent a strand of thinking in British culture which remains influential. It is a line of thought only exacerbated when in the aftermath of such horrific activities as the destruction of the World Trade Center, religion is either lambasted as a whole, or a particular religion – in this case Islam – is too easily misrepresented and vilified. Whether such opposition is willing to make a distinction between religion and spirituality need not detain us here. Letter-writers and commentators who adopt such thinking simply regard the whole lot as hocus-pocus.

There is an argument worth engaging in here. Religion deserves to receive such opposition because of its own sordid past (and, no doubt, the sordid aspects of its future). But it does not deserve to be squeezed out of human culture because of its failures. Its failures, after all, merely serve to show what most religions claim in some form: that humans are limited, did not create the world, and cannot (ultimately) control it, however great their responsibility clearly is to look after it. Limited humans have done limited things in the name of religion. With many years of hindsight the bad things sometimes become clear. Good things become clear too, though.

In a time of 'spirituality boom', religions have a task to help shape those spiritualities, to show where the roots of some seemingly new ideas lie, to argue with each other about the nature of reality, whilst drawing on the rich traditions of faith and thought that each religion has carried with it through time.

Christianity has to re-define and re-present itself in twenty-first-century Britain.

Christianity's own current role takes shape within this 'spirituality boom', and within the need for longstanding religions to re-assert themselves. But the notion of Christianity 're-asserting itself' might sound alarming. To cautious, reserved British ears it might sound like a call for a British Moral Majority movement, or a new wave of Christian fundamentalism, as if the only way that Christianity could re-assert itself was through stubborn, single-minded bolshiness with little leeway for variation in thought and practice amongst Christians themselves. Needless to say, this is not the kind of re-assertion I have in mind.

The re-assertion and re-presentation of Christianity in British society needs to have a number of facets to it. First, those who are Christian need to undertake some basic education in their own tradition. By being more clued-up as to their own faith tradition, they are then better placed to make practical use of it in their lives, and more able to speak to others about it, and its usefulness. Second, churches need to be less timid in going public about the issues with which they wrestle, and with the means by which they tackle such issues. We apologize too much for having religion. We need to be prepared to show that we regard it as a perfectly normal way of living. Third, the media need to acknowledge religion much more as a feature of human living. I watch too many chat-shows for my own good. I am amazed at how little philosophy and religion is touched upon, even when interviewers seem to be priding themselves on 'digging deep' into their interviewees' lives, and when interviewees themselves offer clues to values and beliefs that they live by. It is as if asking people what beliefs they live by is more personal, and always less interesting, than asking who they've slept with.

In this context, those who are responsible for presenting Christian faith in a variety of settings – as teachers, lecturers, preachers, pastors – need to be less reserved about acknowledging the contemporary viability of holding a Christian faith. Admittedly, different concrete contexts require different types of presentation. A seminary is not a university. But gone are the days when the latter can claim objectivity and neutrality. The difference between a seminary or theological college course (in which it is assumed that a confessing view of a religion is going to be propounded) and a university (where no particular confession should be espoused) is a matter of degree, not kind. The former must also consider alternatives respectfully, and its own tradition critically. The latter must accept the limitations and ideological persuasions of its teachers, together with the constraints of academic fashion. But in both educational contexts, and in the life of churches, it should be more possible than often occurs at present for the sheer contemporary viability of holding to, and living by, Christian faith to be made plain.

Of course, this summons to re-definition, re-assertion and fresh presentation says nothing about what form of Christianity should be proposed. The detailed answer to that question lies even beyond the scope of this book.[3] But that a more upbeat, optimistic approach could be adopted is clear.

The place of a religion (e.g., Christianity) in a person's life in twenty-first-century Britain has to be made more plausible.

It is not, however, just a matter of establishing and arguing for Christianity's contemporary viability, as if Christianity remained 'out there' as some abstract phenomenon. The contemporary viability has to be translated into workable religion. This is not mere pragmatism, or utilitarianism. Christianity is not being reduced to what works or what makes people happy or comfortable. But it is about accepting the fact that if Christianity is going to be shown to be viable, then it has to be shown how it works, and how it connects with the lives that people lead. It will not, in other words, be enough to assert that Christianity remains an option in the midst of the many spiritualities on offer. Nor will it be sufficient to propose that well-established Christian practices (e.g., baptism, marriage, holy communion), beliefs (in God, Christ, the Holy Spirit) or theological ideas (justification by faith, sanctification, kingdom of God) can be shown to have a meaning even now. Both of these approaches will need to be carried through. But the challenge will remain to show *how* they cut ice in the everyday world. For too long, and in too many contexts, Christians have assumed it sufficient to carry on asserting their grasp of truth to each other, or from their bunkers to the wider world. The next chapter will offer a reading of different discussions as to how Christian theology can be used to address this issue.

There can be no dodging of the question of whether there is an 'absolute religion'.

It may, however, be good to argue that the mainstream religions are worth re-asserting. And it may well then be appropriate to suggest that Christianity re-assert itself. But does this mean that all religions do the same in parallel? Does such an approach assume the essential equality of religions? Does it even presuppose the identity of their content and direction? It is here where the full significance of the attention given to religious pluralism in recent years takes effect. The fruits of such attention, reflected in the discussion starters to follow, are the result not just of meetings of minds, but of encounters between people.

Inter-faith dialogue in recent years has largely moved beyond the assumption that all religions are saying the same thing. There has also been a tendency towards acknowledging that religions really are quite distinct and 'particular'. But if the latter course is taken too far, it becomes impossible to speak of humanity as a whole. All we have left are different traditions and world-views pertaining to different groups of people, who are unable to speak to other groups. (We shall need to look at this more in the next chapter.)

This means that religions really do compete with each other. They compete with each other in respect of reality and truth. All are trying to offer people a set of practices within which to live their lives. And most offer those practices on the basis of a metaphysical framework, that is, a reading of what really is, within above and beyond the material world in which we live. But it would be intellectually lazy to assume that all are essentially the same. Despite common areas of interest and many agreements, they often really are saying very different things. And it would be morally irresponsible to suggest that religions can simply be left in parallel, without any interaction, as if different versions of truth and different courses of action were a matter of indifference.

There is, then, no dodging the question of whether there is an 'absolute religion'. In other words, it is necessary to ask whether one of the current religions, or a possible future religion yet to emerge out of those currently available, might not have greater recourse to truth than all others.

We don't have the grounds to conclude what an 'absolute religion' might be.

The problem is: we don't seem to be able to state with any certainty what such an 'absolute religion' might look like. Nor can we take up a standpoint, in relation to those religions with which we are familiar, to be able to say which is best. We have to ask the question (which seems to be best?) but we don't have sufficient information to answer it.

Religions thus have to live alongside each other, with different outlooks and practices, knowing that each is concerned with matters and realities which lie beyond their own people, practices, ideas and beliefs. No religion, however, has a full grasp on reality. None can be reduced to some notional 'absolute' lying beyond it. At the same time, none can forgo the question of how absolutes/the Absolute might relate to its practices and beliefs. Religions thus live in as much uncertainty and unclarity as any other movements. But it is part of their *raison d'être* to resist the notion that the question of absolutes is a non-question.

Thus, whilst there may be no absolute religion, there can be no religion worth its name which is not concerned with absoluteness. And whilst religions must be concerned with absolutes and the Absolute, a religion errs when it claims it has found it.

Concluding that we don't know what an 'absolute religion' might look like does not validate 'pick-and-mix' spirituality, or imply that participation in a religion is a matter of indifference.

Religious pluralism is a fact of life. There are many religions, and it would, at the very least, be unwise to suggest that plurality should be reduced to a single religion. At its worst, a claim for such reduction would amount to religious fascism. Limitless plurality, however, would not be commendable either, for the simple reason that not every form of professed religion can be claimed to be a good thing.[4] Between two undesirable extremes, then, concern for an 'absolute religion' finds its appropriate place. However, concern for 'the absolute religion' is more of a conceptual strategy than a realistic hope of being able to conclude an absolute concrete form for religious belief. Because plurality will always be with us, no absolute religion will be found. Because limitless plurality is morally indefensible, a concern for truth and absolutes must remain.

Dialogue, disagreement, even argument will remain, then, part of the future picture for religions. The challenge is how to conduct such dialogue without violence or war.

The rediscovery of religion is a global phenomenon.

At this point, the limited nature of a West-only approach to religion becomes clear. The desire to re-assess the religious climate and to suggest a re-assertion of religion in the West may seem a quaint proposal harking back to a golden age. It may seem inappropriate at the start of the twenty-first century. But such a view would be strangely parochial in a global age. Religion appears to be of little social and political consequence only in the West, and in those parts of the world influenced by the West. To address again the question of the viability of holding a religious faith in western culture, and to do so in a post-modern, post-atheist age, is simply respecting what many cultures outside the West would encourage us to do.

The rediscovery of religion has its dangers.

The global context, however, provides us with ample evidence also of the dangers of rediscovering religion. Not all religion is good religion. And precisely because religion touches the deepest of human concerns, and cannot be a matter of indifference, it is closely implicated in many of the world's so-called 'trouble spots' (Ireland, former Yugoslavia, Israel–Palestine, Tibet, and Afghanistan). Furthermore, much of the religion which appears strong in many parts of the world is of an intolerant kind (e.g., some forms of Irish and North American Protestant Christianity, a form of Islam in Afghanistan). At this point, one cannot but have sympathy with the agnostic or atheist critics of religion to be found throughout the West. War and religion often do go hand in hand.

The challenge here is how to respect the fact that religion has its dangers, and propose a fresh reception and exploration of religion in the West in the light of the North West's own history, without implying a new form of western imperialism. What, in other words, can be learned from the recent period of western history, which has demonstrated a distinct coolness towards religion, in such a way that it is not simply implied that (still) 'West knows best'?

Much of the new energy in Christianity as a world religion comes from outside the (North) West.

One of the main means by which the 'West knows best' assumption can be qualified is through the recognition that so much of the new energy in Christianity derives from outside the West. Christianity in Africa, Latin America, and Asia has produced many new forms of Christianity from which the West has learned, and will continue to learn. For many years now, the notion of the West 'sending missionaries' to the rest of the world has been under serious challenge. It still goes on, and is misguided when not seen in the light of Christianity's missionary endeavours being closely allied with colonial expansion. Missionary activity across the world is now much better seen as 'mission partnership'. As a result of this, contact, exchange and interchange between Christian workers across the world brings rich rewards for individuals and churches, and new insights into the ways that Christianity is formed, re-formed and interacts with different cultures.

It would be wrong, though, to overlook the ways in which such missionary activity past and present creates for contemporary Christianity a continuing set of fresh challenges. Cultural interaction and 'learning from the wider Christian world' is not easy. We would be deluding ourselves if we thought that however central our Christianity might be to our lifestyle, we did not work out our Christian faith in conjunction with other frameworks for viewing reality. Because we are all constrained by our own cultures, and must also work within some form of belief and truth framework alongside which our Christian faith takes shape, basic questions such as 'What is Christianity?', 'Who is God?' and 'What is truth?' are still posed within given cultural frameworks. To give a very concrete example: as a Westerner admittedly influenced by rationalism, I remain puzzled at how easily some western Christians can report (as a criticism of the lack of faith of western churches) that 'resurrections are happening everyday in Africa'. I have to admit my lack of belief at this point. I simply don't believe that people are actually dying and being brought back to life.[5] This does not mean that I am not in the process of learning much from African Christians – about the scale of what one can expect God to achieve in the world, for example. But it does mean that there are always points where it is not enough to speak simply of 'you have your culture and I have mine'. Granted, it may be regarded a matter of imposing western rationalism to ask for verification of what is being claimed. On the other hand, such an example becomes a good test case for where cultures and assumptions clash, and yet where they may be a way of moving forward towards a new truth (about what is actually happening in such cases, and about what 'resurrection' is meant to mean).

*   *   *

This second chapter has focused upon the religious context within which any argument for the viability of taking religion seriously in Britain has to be formulated. I have also begun to look at what, specifically, would need to be considered if anyone were to look at Christianity as a plausible channel through which to be religious in British society today. In the chapters to follow, the plausibility of such an option will be unpacked in more detail.

Available Resources, Persistent Traditions: The Theological Context

This chapter is an important part of the argument, for it's about the movements in Christian thought and practice upon which my case rests. But not everyone likes to deal with foundations or 'background stuff'. Or at least, some readers may not want to face such material at this stage. You may prefer to see where the argument heads first, before coming back to the material here. If so, that's fine. But I hope you will return to this chapter, for if you don't, then you won't really fully understand 'where I'm coming from'. And a satisfactory engagement with what I'm up to throughout this book really requires you to look both at where I end up (Chapters 4 to 6), as well as how I get there (Chapters 2 and 3). If you do decide to keep this chapter on hold for the time being, then it would be worth your while at least looking through first the list of discussion starters which the chapter contains (see Appendix 1, numbers 31–41) before you proceed with Chapter 4.

We all stand within an assortment of 'traditions', because if we didn't, we wouldn't be human.

No religion is rootless. Even so-called New Religious Movements relate or react to existing religions. No form of religiosity is rootless. Some contemporary spiritualities may appear to be free-floating, wholly aloof from structures, liberated from the socio-psychological hassles of human organization. But even this is only apparent. And where spiritualities thrive on their individualism and prove to be escapist (as opposed, say, to mystical), they merely deny their roots and do a disservice to their proponents.

Religion is not being reduced to basic laws of social psychology if we note that they function like other movements of thought and practice. Whatever else religions prove to be, they are human movements which comprise sets of practices, implying assumptions about human beings and the world. They produce bodies of literature (Scriptures) and other material (stories, myths, liturgies) which carry, and sometimes explicitly articulate, these assumptions. When God/the divine is involved, then these assumptions are properly called 'theological'.

Even if people aren't theologically 'religious', however, they will nevertheless be living within a tradition, or a variety of traditions, whether or not they are aware of the fact. We all have stories that we live by. In this sense, then, religions are simply one particular form of the 'stories people live by'. For religious people, their stories (and traditions, Scriptures, practices, myths, liturgies) are likely to be the most significant ones in their lives. It is therefore not surprising that they want others to live by them, or that they get rather defensive when these highly significant stories are critiqued or insulted.

In setting out, then, to clarify which particular understanding of tradition and traditions we are operating with within Christianity, we are not doing anything very unusual. We are merely being very specific about the styles of Christian thought and practice which appear to be helpful in Britain in the present.

It is crucial to know which traditions you stand in.

The previous point suggests something further: that it would be very useful for readers to try and determine which traditions they stand in before proceeding any further. The first chapter will have encouraged readers to take a first step in this direction (What politics, religion, understanding of family do you live by? What 'isms' shape your life, positively and negatively?). Here, in particular, if you have stood, or now stand, in any specific religious tradition, then it is worth bringing it explicitly to mind. Sometimes, such an exercise can be an excuse for pigeon-holing, or abusive-labelling. Saying 'he's an evangelical' or 'she's a liberal' can prevent people truly meeting and listening to each other. But labels can be important if they mean something, are owned, and thus function as self-descriptors. In this sense 'labels' are but shorthand ways of identifying the traditions in which we stand. One of the saddest, and most problematic, aspects of Christianity in Britain today is that those within it often understand all too little about the labels they claim for themselves, or use of others.

In what follows I shall admittedly be risking elements of stereotyping. But as I explore mostly the positive aspects of each style of Christianity (and largely leave readers to read between the lines as to the weaknesses of each), I trust this will be helpful.

From the catholic tradition we learn the importance of church order and of liturgy.

By 'catholic tradition' here I do not, of course, simply mean Roman Catholicism. The Roman Catholic theologian Avery Dulles has offered five possible definitions of the word 'catholic'. I am using his fourth definition here: 'The type of Christianity that attaches particular importance to visible continuity in space and time and visible mediation through social and institutional structures, such as creeds, sacraments, and the historic episcopate.'[1] On this understanding, we can readily identify catholic Baptists, Methodists, and Anglicans, as well as catholic Roman Catholics. 'Catholicism', above all, thus accepts the inevitability of the Church structuring its life. The structure of its life – primarily in its liturgical life (so that worship is not undertaken shoddily) and the ordering of its ministries (so that appropriate people are authorized to do identifiable jobs) – is seen as crucial not simply to the smooth running of an organization, but as an aid to the health and wholeness of Christianity in any age.

Most styles of Christianity have their 'catholic' elements, even the most anti-(Roman) Catholic. The very fact that some kind of order is needed in worship and in the organization of Christian culture means that even the most 'free' of churches has catholic traits. Pastors of 'free' churches are often very clear about who's in charge. 'Free worship' often follows a set (even if not written) pattern. These examples simply remind us that familiarity and regularity of structure can, in fact, be liberating. Set orders of worship do not need too much thought, and do not induce anxiety amongst regular worshippers (What's going to come next?). People are released to worship through habitual participation. The habits are not the end. They are the liberating means to a worshipful end.

At their best, catholic models of ministry fulfil a similar function.

They encourage less attention than some other understandings of ministry to the individuals occupying the role. Usually allied to a sense that those in ministry *are* ministers, and are not merely *doing the job* of a minister, catholic understandings especially emphasize the extent to which ministers are channels of divine grace. Even if some may bridle at the apparently inevitable hierarchy implicit in this approach to church ministry, it recognizes two things: the need for the work of God to be channelled in embodied form in the world; and, somewhat paradoxically, the need to counter overemphasis upon the individuals who carry the responsibility for being God's representatives.[2] Individualism is played down further through ministers/priests all wearing a similar 'clerical uniform'. When seen as less a matter of status and more a badge of office, clerical dress works in favour of the role of priest/minister/pastor enabling communication to occur between believer/searcher/person in need and God.

In the present climate of post-modern fragmentation in Britain, it is scarcely surprising that Christianity is sometimes being found to be attractive in its very ordered, liturgical forms. Liturgies provide shape in a shapeless world. When incorporating ancient forms, and when cultivating a sense of mystery, liturgies supply missing dimensions in a functional world. Where the catholic style of Christianity struggles sharply at present is in the loss of social role and status of the Christian minister in British society. At a time of numerical decline and decreasing socio-political impact, when churches are part of the service industry (with regard to births, marriages and deaths), the relative anonymity of clergy is less to do with human beings decreasing in significance, so that knowledge of God may abound, and more a matter of their joining the ranks of nameless functionaries who make society work.

From Radical Orthodoxy we learn of the contemporary importance of liturgy, in the context of a trenchant critique of modernity's influence upon Christianity.

'Radical Orthodoxy' is a specific, contemporary form of resurgent catholic tradition. It is also a form of post-liberalism (see later in this chapter). Drawing heavily both on Anglo-Catholicism and the catholic form of Christian Socialism, the movement offers a severe

*Now Prof –
Manchester*

critique of late-twentieth-century accommodations to liberal politics and secular models for understanding society and religion. Various arguments from quite different supporters of Radical Orthodoxy are offered in favour of, for example, a re-asserted Christian framework for human living (John Milbank), liturgy as a way of structuring the whole of life (Catherine Pickstock), and the human body as a necessary focus for theological reflection (Graham Ward). Each of these writers takes something specific out of the traditions from which Radical Orthodoxy draws and offers a distinct contribution to Radical Orthodoxy's own development. In so doing, they also demonstrate the extent to which Radical Orthodoxy is itself a child of its time, tapping into so many contemporary currents of thought and belief.[3]

of st. Cath.

First and foremost, Radical Orthodoxy is deeply critical of individualistic, liberal modernism. In this sense, it is post-modern. It looks for a corporate reading of Christian faith (in its stress on catholicism, liturgy and socialism). Second, its emphasis upon the communal dimension of Christianity contains an emphasis upon embodiment. Catholic and Christian Socialist concerns for the material are found clearly in Radical Orthodoxy. It does not in any sense seek to reduce Christianity to the material. But it relates directly to contemporary hesitancy about the immaterial and the spiritual in human life in the way it seeks to re-locate the focus of what it means to be religious in the midst of material concerns (about sexuality, friendship, music, cities, violence, art).

Radical Orthodoxy is a bold set of voices. It will almost certainly be a short-lived movement as it stands. Its leading writers, having been Cambridge-based, have, on the whole, dispersed, and – despite the wonders of modern technology – it remains true that people usually still need to meet in embodied form to make a movement work. But its emphases are helpful, stark reminders of some of the issues that need to be at the forefront of the re-assertion of Christianity in the West. Christianity may well have learned much, and yet have much to learn, from the modern period in western culture, from the rise of the human individual since the Renaissance, and even from the triumph of capitalist economics. Radical Orthodoxy offers one form of the necessary resistance, however, to the inevitable assumption that such western emphases should dominate the way we understand the world to work.

Radical Orthodoxy is also rather esoterically presented. Its writers

I wish the various authors like Catherine Pickstock would write more intelligible!

offer their thoughts in opaque language in a manner that is somewhat out of keeping with the Socialist strand of Christian thought
upon which they draw. As a movement it is a reminder that if
Christianity is to have a practical resurgence in Britain, then its
emphases, in contemporary forms, have to be offered in a compre-
hensible as well as a plausible way.

And that goes for some in liberalism too.

Liberalism shows how it is possible to remain a religious believer within the post-Enlightenment world.

It is very easy to knock liberalism in all its many forms. Liberal
morals are the butt of conservative critics. Liberal economics receive
criticism from political left-wingers and right-wingers alike. Liberal
religion is assumed to lead to a relativistic free-for-all in which no
one believes very much any more. All these scenarios do liberalism
an injustice.

In Christian terms, liberalism means a critical strand of modern
thinking and belief from the end of the eighteenth century through
to the late twentieth century. Its beginnings in European Protestantism
are found in the work of Friedrich Schleiermacher.[4] Schleiermacher's
strategy was to expound Christianity in relation to facets of the
human condition which he hoped everyone in his thought world
(western Europe) would be able to recognize. For this bold attempt
he is frequently castigated by his critics for reducing theology to
anthropology, and turning worship of God into worship of the
human self. The Enlightenment 'turn to the human subject', as a
result of which human being became the measure of all things, is
seen, in Schleiermacher, to reach its apotheosis. Nothing could be
further from the truth.

Schleiermacher started a trend in modern Christian (especially
Protestant) thought which undoubtedly led to followers wandering
up some cul-de-sacs. But given his time, and the place in which he
worked, he himself could do no other in seeking to be an apologist
for Christianity. He and the liberal traditions in Christian thought
which trace their origins back to him have thus contributed much to
the very survival of a viable Christianity in the modern and post-
modern periods. It is not the human that is worshipped in liberal
Christian thought. What is sought is a version of Christianity which
(allowing, as we can now see, for different cultural constraints) any

human being can access. In contemporary terms: the liberal tradition continues to set a challenge to Christianity to relate directly to whatever understandings of the human being are operative in the cultures in which we live and work.

Liberal traditions have allowed contemporary life-experience to exert a strong influence upon the way the various themes of Christian theology (God, Christ, Church, spirit) should be understood. In keeping with the spirit of the Reformation, they have been willing to be critical of what the Church taught. They have been open to new truth from wherever it came, making them prone to the charge that they have allowed non-Christian frameworks of thought to pass judgement on Christianity. Experience, criticism, openness: these are hallmarks and strengths of liberal traditions. Without them, I contend, there is not much hope of offering an argument for Christianity's viability in contemporary Britain.

Liberalism has understandably had its opponents. Stress human experience too much, and you end up worshipping human beings. Look to your own experience as the measure of all things, and you end up worshipping yourself. Be critical constantly, and you're in danger of having no fixed traditions to work with. And where are you standing to be critical at all? Be ever open to all, and you're in danger of implying that nothing really matters. Taken to its extreme, the only ultimate value is complete, relativistic individualism. None of these positions would have been supported by Schleiermacher. To put them together in this kind of way offers a parody of liberalism. Yet liberalism has not always been aware of some of the dangerous tendencies of its emphases.

Even Barth was very sympathetic to Schleiermacher even if he rejected him. ✓

Post-liberalism re-asserts the corporate nature of Christianity, the crucial role of the Church and the importance of narrative in Christian belief and practice.

After liberalism, logically, comes 'post-liberalism'. Forming itself as a movement in contemporary Christian theology since about the early 1980s, post-liberalism locates itself by its very name in relation to the liberalism it so severely criticizes. Summarized quintessentially in the work of the American Lutheran theologian George Lindbeck, post-liberalism offers what is called a 'cultural-linguistic' way of looking at how Christian theology works.[5] Post-liberalism in fact opposes both traditionalist dogmatics (which started with 'propositions') and also the approach of liberal traditions (which were 'experientially expressivist' in that they encouraged people to express their experience). Its cultural-linguistic model accepts that when people use religious language, they are not merely speaking of their experience. They are relating to a given tradition, a tradition which is already 'there', embodied in the beliefs and practices of a concrete community of people (Church). Being a Christian is thus like learning a language. You live within a culture (the culture of Christianity), are a member of a community (a church), and pick up a set of words (liturgy, theological language) within which to live your life. *This can be applied more widely.*

All of this means that religious people live within a distinct world-view. It is different from those of other religious traditions and philosophies, who will relate to different communities and learn different languages. Different Christians will even relate to distinct communities and languages (or perhaps we should say dialects), even when they seem to be speaking the same language. As an approach to Christian theology, post-liberalism thus tends more to promote the 'religions in parallel' approach rather than any view which would easily foster dialogue between religions. It accepts diversity, but raises profound questions about the ease with which any religion or philosophy may communicate with any other. Translation may happen. But it may be more difficult than is often supposed. We cannot assume, as some liberals have so often done, that behind all religions and world-views lies the same basic humanity which, when articulated by distillation from those religions and world-views, will be identical. In contrast to such an assumption, post-liberalism argues for the irreducibility of religions. Religions are not dispensable husks surrounding a kernel of human experience. Because traditions are so vital in human living, there is a sense in which we *are* the traditions we live.

Post-liberalism is probably the most important corrective to the liberalism which has been in the ascendant for many phases of Christian theology throughout the modern period. It marks a major corrective not just to modern liberalism, but to the many tendencies to promote the importance of human experience (especially individual experience) over and above the traditions carried by the Church. It also re-asserts the vital importance of churches as real, embodied, living communities of contemporary believers, without which there would be no Christian theology at all. Furthermore, it looks closely at the *forms* in which Christian beliefs are usually carried, noting that religion uses story rather than proposition as a main vehicle for carrying the truth by which it lives. This insight, too, has been of profound significance in recent Christian theology. Theologians prone to speaking solely in propositions and dogmatic assertions have been caught on the hop somewhat through this reminder of the difference between real religion and theological tradition.

But post-liberalism has weaknesses. It is so keen to critique liberalism's emphasis on human experience that it plays down how important it must be to relate religious faith to that experience. Liberalism did not emphasize experience out of laziness, due to a lack of understanding of religion, or in order to worship humanity instead of God. It did so because it saw that religion really did help people to understand their experience better and to live differently, and because it was keen that more people interpret their lives in this religious way. Mission and social change went hand in hand. Second, post-liberalism's introversion (you have to be inside the language, and once you get inside it, it seems to be assumed that you stay there) seems dangerously ghetto-like. It encourages neither dialogue nor mission. At root, post-liberalism is a retreating, defensive form of Christianity which is comfortable as a minority movement, or as an expression of a self-satisfied clique. It may appeal that it is humble and modest. But it is not the theological approach of a movement which seriously thinks that it is in possession of some insights into a God who is interested in the whole world. *I don't like it much!*

(*y. the world. A Stanley Hauerwas in Ellius*)

The charismatic and pentecostal movements keep alive in Christianity the dangerous memory of the workings of the spirit of God throughout the world.

Most branches of Christianity have struggled with those members who have wanted to stress the workings of the spirit of God. Western forms of Christianity, Protestantism especially, have sat more comfortably with an emphasis upon Father and Son, rather than Spirit, upon word rather than spirit, and even upon word as opposed to action or visible embodiment. Eastern forms of Christianity have always challenged this (mis)emphasis, as have many uprisings (revivals) within western Christianity itself. It would be nice to think that western Christianity might yet learn from those uprisings within itself, as well as other Christian voices from without.

'Pentecostal' forms of Christianity relate to Pentecost, the time at which, in the account of early Christianity found in the New Testament in the book of Acts (in Acts 2.1–42), a kind of special imparting and reception of God's Holy Spirit was experienced by the first Christians. The apostles were especially inspired to preach in a way that enabled people who spoke in other languages to under-stand. From the Acts account, it is clear that for the apostles this 'reception' of the spirit was a highly charged affair, a moving and emotionally powerful occurrence. 'Charismatic' Christianity can refer to the same forms of Christianity, though usually adds an extra dimension, focusing upon the 'gifts' (charismata) of the spirit as listed by the early Christian apostle Paul in his first letter to the Christians in Corinth (1 Cor. 12.4–11). Both such forms of Christianity are thus distinctly 'biblical' in the sense that there is early, scriptural support for the style of Christianity being promoted.

This is itself one of the great strengths of these styles of Christianity. They stand as a challenge to all forms of Christianity to demonstrate the extent to which, and ways in which, they are in continuity with the earliest Christian movements. They press, in particular, the ways in which much early Christianity was clearly powerfully dynamic, and touched every aspect of human living: not just the head, not just the heart, but the whole human spirit and body. Encounter with God is seen to shake people to the core and affect their whole being. It affects every different type of human activity. In this, the non-rational – but not necessarily irrational – aspects of both humanity and religion are respected.

Teaching, preaching, and health care are all mentioned directly by Paul. We would now want to add: financial management, personnel work, engineering, medical science, entertainment and, above all, the arts. These are, after all, activities which profoundly affect how human and natural resources are managed, how life is interpreted, and how human creativity is discovered and expressed. Charismatic and pentecostal forms of Christianity thus challenge constantly any desire to confine to a discrete area of life the working of God.

Their weakness is that they often fail to achieve precisely what their emphasis has the potential to do. Like the forms of Christianity they so rightly criticize, they too become styles of Christianity which confine the working of God's spirit to churches. They too 'routinize' into accepted patterns the seemingly unruly, empowering, dispersed spirit of God at work in the wider world. Through over-emphasis upon specific forms of 'Christian ministry', the words of Paul are not translated into contemporary terms, other than as the rationale for a particular current form of ecclesiastical organization (usually centred around pastors, preachers, healers, youth leaders, and prophets).

But other styles of Christianity mock charismatic and prophetic forms at their peril. For too much criticism, or a failure to recognize the important emphases of these forms, merely confirms the extent to which other styles of Christianity are deficient.

No Rocking but How les tote criticism as the Westens well knew.

Evangelicalism emphasizes personal faith, Jesus-centredness and the sovereign action of God.

Many styles of Christianity could be grouped under the heading of evangelicalism. I am using three main sub-themes in order to try and encapsulate evangelicalism's main focal points: personal faith, Jesus-centredness and the sovereign action of God. By 'personal faith' I simply mean that evangelicalism stresses that believers need to make Christian faith their own. Though most forms of evangelicalism are also highly 'propositional' (in the sense that people are clearly expected to believe certain things, and to be able to state these beliefs in the form of statements or propositions), it is clear that the belief itself is insufficient. Evangelicals look to believers to internalize their beliefs and live by them. In this way, it is easy to see how and why evangelical Christianity is 'individualistic' in being 'personal'. It has contributed to, or been an expression of, the individualistic modernism which much contemporary thought so opposes.

Evangelicalism is also 'Jesus-centred'. Jesus is central to evangelical Christianity: as the one who secured redemption, as the one upon whom all Christian life should be modelled, even as the one to whom we should pray. Push this emphasis very far, however, and it becomes clear that more enquiry is needed. 'Jesus-centred' will need to mean 'God-centred'. And 'Jesus-centred' will often not mean simply 'the centrality of the teachings of Jesus of Nazareth'. There is, in other words, much which is left unspoken in this emphasis.[6]

*Mr Jebbreston gives - Cross aurhw. Evargelin.
- Conversion.
- activism.*

However, as an emphasis it is emotively and devotionally powerful and has fuelled so much evangelical spirituality in the past two centuries.

Being 'Jesus-centred' equates with being 'God-centred' precisely because the action of God is summed up in the life, death and resurrection of Jesus. The sheer, supreme controlling hand of God is seen at work in Jesus. This is the pinnacle of God's action throughout history. Nothing can stop God doing what God wants to do. God will act graciously and lovingly, but can do all things. There can be no sense in which God's action is limited.

When placed under these three headings 'evangelicalism' can encompass many groups. It could include what may be called 'orthodox-reformed' versions of Christianity (relating to Presbyterianism, Congregationalism, the United Reformed Church, and some Free Evangelical Churches). Some might now express discomfort, though, with some of the directions taken by post-Reformation versions of 'Jesus-centredness'. The welcome attention upon the doctrine of the Trinity has asked some awkward questions of evangelicalism and Reformed Christianity at this point. Be that as it may, evangelicalism in its many forms has contributed powerful currents into western Christianity through these three emphases. The first has latched on to the emotional power of Christian belief. The second emphasis has made use of the accessibility of God in and through people giving attention to the figure of Jesus (historically, and as carried culturally and within Christian belief). The third has drawn upon, and furthered, Christian awareness of human limitation.

Liberation theologies have contributed to the questioning of privatized, individualistic forms of Christianity, and have challenged Christians to look at the social and material aspects of Christian faith in God.

If evangelicalism has fed off, and fostered, individualistic forms of Christianity, then liberation theologies have opposed them. Various forms of Christian theology and practice have emerged in the last four decades, outside and inside western Christianity, which have taken theology in new directions, largely through reminding Christianity of hidden or suppressed traditions. 'Liberation theology' is the term often given to the political theologies emerging out of

Latin America since the 1960s. These have been forms of theology which have looked directly at the concerns of the materially poor, and sought to read the Bible and reflect on its contents from the perspective of the poor. As a result, such reflection has proved a major challenge to churches throughout the First World. First World churches have often undertaken their theology, and continued their Christian practice, with little thought to the economic base from which they begin, or to the political, military and economic activity of the states of which they are a part.

A range of other forms of liberation theology – including feminist theology, Black theology, womanist theology, queer theology – have emerged more recently. Each of these forms begins the process of Christian thinking from the perspective of an identifiable group of people. As *liberation* theologies, these processes of reflection are not simply the self-expression of any group. By definition, the group perspective must be that of an oppressed group. An injustice is identified and understood to be anathema to a God who hates injustice. Furthermore, such theologies are not merely processes of reflection. The reflection undertaken must always be linked to action. Analysis and critique is but part of a process of working towards the liberation of the group out of whose perspective the theology is undertaken.

Liberation theologies have thus fed into recent developments in Christian theology a profound concern for concreteness and practical action. As an antidote to a comfortable Christianity, serving the therapeutic well-being of an individual believer (existing in splendid isolation) liberation theologies press for the cash value of religious belief in the real terms of everyday life. They have found wanting many forms of western Christianity, and challenged westerners to think more about the consequences of their beliefs and actions upon those in their own societies and beyond. Admittedly, some aspects of Latin American liberation theology's use of Marxism have been subjected to criticism. The optimism of its use of Marxist analysis may need some revision in the light of political and economic developments in Eastern Europe. A further critique is that liberation theologies attract activists who demonstrate little time for reflection. This may, however, prove to be a problem of the activists who operate in this way rather than a problem with liberation theologies themselves. Even if actions do speak louder than words, true liberationists far from deny that words have power.

**Denominations are far from dead and are likely to continue in
some form. But the primary Christian groupings in the future
may be theological movements and spiritual traditions.**

I have chosen to present the variety of Christian theology and
practice in terms of movements and styles rather than denominations. This is, of course, only one way in which Christianity can be
characterized in all its diversity. Arguably, Christian diversity is best
presented through its different branches (Roman Catholicism,
Eastern Orthodoxy, Reformed Christianity, Anglicanism, Methodism, etc.) as this would be more true to its historical flow. That I
have chosen to handle matters differently is simply because it is less
clear than it once was that 'denominations' are either closely defined
or as meaningful to current and potential Christians in Britain.

Having said this, Christianity cannot escape its institutional
forms past and present. Think of Christianity, and you think of
churches. Think of churches and you think of buildings. Find those
buildings, and you'll see that they have labels (Baptist, United
Reformed Church, Pentecostal Church, Church of England). Those
labels indicate the existence of very different institutional shapes,
but they are institutions nevertheless, with organizational structures, leadership battles, power bases, budgets, plans and strategies.
Christianity in Britain is still, inevitably, affected deeply by those
structures. Denominations are far from dead.

Nor should the importance of denominations be downplayed.
The fact that I have concentrated on theological movements and
styles in no way indicates that I think denominations have no present or future value. They do and will have value. It is, though, clear
that Christianity will not again become a living channel through
which people live their lives in Britain through emphasis upon
denominational labels. It is not as Methodists or Baptists or
Anglicans that people will be persuaded that Christianity is worth
considering. People will be persuaded to consider Christianity as a
viable religion option for a whole variety of reasons (makes sense of
life, provides friends, helps with philosophizing, provides a lead in
political reflection, helps with the inner life, etc.) and they will
then discover what 'being Baptist', 'being Methodist' or 'being a
Reformed Christian' might mean. It is not likely to happen the other
way round. This does not, however, mean that denominational
labels should go out of fashion. On the contrary, one of the weak-

nesses of much Christianity in Britain today is that those *in* particular traditions are not very knowledgeable about those traditions.

Denominations will therefore continue, and will need to continue, as spiritual and theological traditions upon which people of many different styles will draw. Christianity in Britain may even be likely to remain structured, for practical (economic) reasons, on largely denominational lines. The growing number of Local Ecumenical Partnerships which exist may start to challenge this situation. Be that as it may, it is in my view more important for people who need briefing about Christianity first to become clear about Christian diversity via the alternative route I have proposed. Otherwise, the bafflement about how different Christians can be from each other is more likely to remain. Without an awareness of what makes Christians different (through their different emphases), it is unlikely that a bemused enquirer will be able to take any steps towards thinking that Christianity might, after all, have something useful to offer them in Britain today.

This section can thus be read as a counterbalance to the discussion starters with which this chapter began ('We all stand within an assortment of "traditions", because if we didn't, we wouldn't be human' and 'It is crucial to know which traditions you stand in'). We can now see the crucial role played by a variety of Christian traditions. Those who attach themselves to Christianity in any way will stand within one or more Christian traditions. And it's vital that Christians work out what different traditions can offer and achieve. This is part of Christians' clarifying what Christianity is for today, and how it relates, and can relate, to British people and British society.

Christians working with other Christians (ecumenism) is the only way forward. But ecumenism will not mean uniformity. It will mean unity in diversity.

The diversity of Christianity is irreducible. Anyone who pretends that Christianity (in Britain, let alone the world) is likely to be shaped into a single institutional structure is misguided. This does not mean, though, that the search for 'Christian unity' is misplaced. On the contrary, Christians working with other Christians (especially where those Christians have some marked differences between them) is surely one of the best forms of Christian mission that exists.

Nor does it mean that some forms of Christianity (even in institutional form) might not prove more commendable than others. Diversity for diversity's sake, however, is profoundly mistaken, misrepresents the God in whom Christians believe, and ultimately feeds the individualism which has been so corrosive in western culture. Some in the ecumenical movement have, however, found it both easier and more creative to speak about the quest for 'visible' rather than 'organic' unity. In other words: work with others, and be seen to work with others. But don't pretend that it's either right or possible for all to be contained within a single structure.

Differences can, after all, be real and require recognition (e.g., ethnic differences, personality types). The main issue at stake, then, is for Christians to determine amongst one another which differences matter more than others, and which should be the cause of a lack of uniformity in Christian theology and practice. This issue is easy to pose in question form. To answer it, of course, takes one to the heart of Christianity itself.

There is, though, one important twist to the ecumenical endeavour. Christians working with other Christians can always sound the right and good thing to be doing, and it surely is. But it can sometimes become a matter of Christians working with Christians in a locality at cost to a sense that Christians are part of a broader religious tradition and a world Church. Such 'inter-church' activities, whilst good, can, in other words, obscure the broader ecumenical task, and idolize the local. This danger will need bearing in mind as we proceed.

* * *

This third chapter has been concerned with the many different emphases which Christians can have. They surface in different theological movements and styles of Christianity. All of those that I have briefly considered are with us today in British Christianity. No single form considered can be held to be 'right' without qualification. All have strengths and weaknesses. In practice, British Christians draw on one or more of these styles (sometimes without even realizing).

In future chapters I shall draw especially on the tensions between liberalism and post-liberalism, and some of the features of evangelicalism. I shall not, however, ignore emphases from other styles and movements. What is more, I shall be drawing together an argument for the particular, continued value of a 'protesting' style of Christianity. Despite my claim that denominationalism is not the best way to characterize Christian diversity, I shall nevertheless want to speak of 'Protestantism'. This is less a denominational label, however (being itself a term which refers to many denominations), and more a way of construing a form of Christianity which makes contemporary sense in Britain.

My own way forward does, of course, reflect personal experience and preference. But it is not simply a matter of presenting 'what worked for me'. I am seeking to present Christianity in an accessible form, without resorting to sheer pragmatism, yet whilst respecting the ways in which it can yet have a huge role to play in the continued transformation of individuals and society in Britain today.

a good survey.

4

A Chastened Liberalism: Towards a Viable Contemporary Form of the Christian Religion in Britain

Christianity in the West is in danger of becoming totally ghettoized.

A series of profound ironies surrounds the situation in which beleaguered British Christianity now finds itself. As we saw in Chapter 2, on the one hand Christians find themselves in a secular society. On the other, they find themselves being left behind in the wake of a spirituality boom. The liberal phase of Christianity seems to have come to an end and the desire to engage with secular culture seems to have been a failure. Post-liberalism has therefore, seemingly rightly, encouraged Christianity to remember that it is, after all, a religion and needs fostering as such. Individualism, having itself been actively promoted by many branches of Christianity, receives savage critique, and not only from Christians. Yet it is not clear that *any* kind of 'communitarian' approach to religion will do. It is with this third irony that our first discussion starter in this chapter begins.

Numerical decline, a sense of weakness, loss of nerve, lack of intellectual and moral clout, are a number of features of contemporary British Christianity which conspire to put British Christians on the defensive. We are in retreat because, more often than not, unless we are the kind of Christians that cannot see two sides to an argument, we do not quite know how to put what we want to say. Or we do not believe that we will be seriously listened to when we do speak. (It is always easier for society at large to deal in sound-bites and black and white versions of complex issues.) Or we have lost confidence ourselves in the usefulness, let alone potential truth, of key beliefs, ideas and practices within which we live and move and have our being.

A crucial point of interaction [*criticism*] between the Christian liberalism which needed critiquing, and the post-liberalism which critiqued it, however, occurs precisely at this point. In recovering a sense that Christianity is a religion, and not first and foremost a social work agency, post-liberalism has set a new agenda for British Christianity. In reminding Christians that, for Christianity to function, they must meet together in real communities, post-liberals have bolstered a new sense that 'being church' is a crucial feature of Christian living. One problem with these correct and much-needed emphases, however, is that they collude with the general weakness and loss of confidence outlined and create a sense of ghettoization. Many Christians seem content to see themselves as an embattled minority group who will never again have much influence. Whatever may have been the weaknesses of the 'secular' meaning of Christianity or the forms of 'secular Christianity' proposed in the past, the sense in which Christianity is meant to interweave with and interpret the whole of life has been lost. Christianity is, however, not meant to be boxed off, or to be shouted encouragingly from the sidelines. Even if this is not what post-liberalism intended, in its attention to separated communities, and the way in which such 'set apart' communities function, it does seem to promote such a view.

Something has to be done, therefore, this side of the post-liberal critique of liberalism in (post-) modern western Christianity, to maintain a sense of the importance of Christianity even in a secularized world, whilst respecting the fact that Christianity needs to recover its role *as religion* in society. The 'Christendom model', according to which Christianity is simply allied to state control and can assume automatic authority and supremacy in any particular nation or empire, has clearly gone as a viable means of religious influence in society. The Reformation has itself contributed to the demise of such a model, especially as appropriated within the political structures of the United States. But it is no less a consequence and long-term achievement of the Reformation to work out how Christianity can, and must, nevertheless be a social and political force. The challenge in the longest term – five hundred years on from Luther's first criticisms of the Church of which he was a part – has proved to be how Christianity's social and political significance may be maintained without being simply allied to political power, and without assuming that it can only be done by individuals of good-will. *Herbert Butterfield would on this?)*

We need a 'new Christian liberalism'.

The consequence of the previous point is straightforward: we need a 'new Christian liberalism'. A new way needs to be found through which Christians in the West can prevent their own ghettoization, without simply being boldly assertive (as if there were no other voice, or as if no other voice mattered), and without accommodating to any and every moral, intellectual or political fashion or whim in society (the nub of the criticism of liberalism in the past).[1]

I should stress: I am talking here of a *theological* liberalism. I mean that there has to be an irreducible diversity in Christian theological thinking and belief. I am not proposing that all liberalisms (political, ethical, economic and educational) are to be accepted as of equal value. Such discussion would take us well beyond the scope of this book. The five 'liberalisms' just referred to naturally inter-weave. But they are not of a piece.[2]

The 'new Christian liberalism' is Christian, because it needs to assert a confidence in the Christian tradition in all its rich variety. It is liberalism because it welcomes the diversity and works with it, in critical continuity in the identifiable strands of Christianity's liberal past. And it is 'new' to signal a fresh departure for those strands in the present and future.

The new Christian liberalism will creatively interact with non-Christian thought forms.

We know we live in a pluralist world. There really are many religions, many political viewpoints, many different views of what constitutes moral high ground. Christians have to be prepared to listen to anybody and everybody in the search for truth. They cannot simply listen to each other. This will not mean that everything will prove of equal value. Nor will it be easy to determine how and what is of most worth. Logically, if you stand in a religious tradition (or any tradition which you deem to be the most significant for your life) then it, and its belief- and value-system, will automatically provide the norms according to which all else will be judged. This will, of course, prove true even for 'new Christian liberals'. What the modern phase of Christianity in particular has shown, however, is just how much of the 'basic world-view' is itself open to change. Massive changes in human knowledge – especially prevalent throughout the post-Enlightenment age – have revealed that Christianity itself shifts in content and meaning, even whilst functioning as the 'basic world-view' for Christians. There is an unavoidable relativity here. And, as we saw in the last chapter, Christianity must increasingly work out its own understanding of itself in critical conversation with other religious traditions, without necessarily assuming any kind of complete and inevitable agreement, even when it is possible to note common ground.

Time has also shown, however, that this does not render the whole edifice of Christianity unstable. Religions go on working despite this. They work because they are not merely intellectual systems. They are sets of beliefs and practices (with stories, habits, communities) which have an intellectual component within them. But because human life itself is not simply a set of cognitive propositions, religions have much work to do beyond the merely rational.

'Creatively interacting with non-Christian thought forms' means being 'interdisciplinary' in the widest sense. Theologians are to learn from sociologists, psychologists, anthropologists, philosophers, linguists, historians and vice versa. They are to learn from, and contribute to, the work of educators, counsellors, community development workers and social workers. They are to interact with the creative output of artists, poets, architects, sculptors, dancers, comedians, film-makers, and novelists.

This has always happened, in fact. We have been less prone to notice this going on throughout much of Christian history because everyone who did any theology included their anthropology, psychology, philosophy (or whatever – though perhaps not too much comedy) within their theology anyway. Since the disciplines have been separated out, there has been a new task to be undertaken (and the philosophers, linguists and anthropologists have not always wanted to serve the interests of religion). And since the caring professions and the arts have increasingly been less linked directly to religion, the useful interaction between them has had to be worked at differently.

The whole process of Christians learning from that which is

outside of Christianity is, though, based on a simple premise. If God is claimed to be creator, then God is creator of all, and all truth is God's truth. To live and work within this belief means to accept the ultimate unity of all that seems to be 'right' and 'true', however partially it may be glimpsed, and however contested our participation in that truth may always have to be.[3]

The new Christian liberalism accepts the critique of liberalism's past tendency to promote individualism.

Individualism is undoubtedly liberalism's Achilles' heel. The perceived need to create space for Christian believers to look critically at their own orthodoxies, and to forge links with ideas and values held by people not Christian, contributed to a growing diversity (fragmentation even) in Christianity throughout the modern period. Anything did seem to go, for a while at least. To remain in a critical continuity with what liberalism was trying to do means acceptance of two principles. First, it means accepting that diversity cannot be limitless, however difficult it may prove to clarify both the parameters of belief and practice, and who should determine these. People cannot simply believe what they want and be Christian. Liberals in the past probably never even actually thought this, but the need for space (freedom!) seemed to imply it at times. Second, therefore, it entails accepting the critique of liberalism's tendency towards promoting an unreserved individualism.

The new Christian liberalism will draw more on Christianity's public role.

The new Christian liberalism will thus be a chastened liberalism, required to accept more the religious, social and political constraints upon the individual which are entailed within a commitment to God as practised in Christian terms. Chastened liberalism will continue to accept the complexity of working out how Christianity can affect individual human lives. However, in resisting some of the options open to Christians, for example, for a Christian to live 'apart from the world', or as society's constant critic, a new Christian liberalism will accept even more responsibly than in the past the public role of Christianity.

In the relatively recent liberal past, it is true that leading British Christians may well have been astute enough to recognize the limits of individualism, and the crucial importance of communal, even institutional, Christian life. In the midst of seeking to try and chart a new course through the 1960s, 70s and 80s, noting the massive socio-political change underway, the need for the Church to change, and the prophetic task required of all Christians, the likes of John A. T. Robinson, David Edwards, David Jenkins and John Habgood can scarcely be accused of disregarding the institutional Church, or of failing to enter into controversial political and ethical realms in their attempt to expound Christian faith on the contemporary scene. But though there are figureheads – leaders of the Church (in this case, the Church of England) – who can be singled out for special mention, the lingering critique of liberalisms of the recent past remains valid: What difference does critical, liberal thinking Christianity make to the public world of the everyday Christian (and thus, potentially, any religiously interested person in Britain today)? Perhaps, as we shall see further in relation to the next discussion starter, we see just how clerical and male-dominated past liberalisms have been.

In practical terms, 'having a more public role' will mean conducting active public discussion, in theological perspective, of the available political options in Britain today. It will mean doing more than providing opportunities for individual Christians to feel 'supported' in their working lives, or to cope (as escapees) with the 'world of work', as if this were another dimension of human existence, set apart from religious practice. Christianity will only have a realistic, connected future for people in Britain when included within it is an active component which enables people to think creatively and critically, in theological perspective, about the work that they do, paid or unpaid, the activities they undertake and the relationships they enjoy.

The new Christian liberalism will build on its known, past commitment to theological education and critical thinking. In so doing, it will again risk the charge of élitism.

The previous insight leads to the stark and challenging conclusion of a threefold agenda: theological education, theological education and theological education.[4] Liberals have, of course, long been accused of seeing education as the solution to all human ills. Too much in the world militates against the wisdom of such a single, simple approach. Not all political and religious conflicts, for example, seem conducive to resolution by calm, considered discourse. (Would that we had tried, and might go on trying.) Education will not solve everything. But despite having so many resources to make Christianity in the West a more informed kind of Christianity, the opportunities have rarely been taken in practice. There is little doubt that Christianity itself could be transformed through its members being better informed about their own faith, its place within the world of faiths, and the society in which these faiths take shape.

In the process of preparing to write this book I looked again at some of the manifestos from the 1960s and 1970s. John Bowden's *Voices in the Wilderness* is a tombstone for a lost age, an age of past hopefulness.[5] Bowden looks back at the potential promise of the 'Honest to God' phase of British Christianity, when it looked (even back then) as though Christianity would not turn into a ghettoized form of religion, and would take on the secular world in a positive yet not uncritical way. Bowden is pessimistic. But his pessimism is understandable when one looks further back at some key works between 1963 and 1977.

John A. T. Robinson's *Honest to God* was one of the very few books of theology to be a million best-seller.[6] It provoked enormous interest and discussion inside and outside the churches. It gave critical believers hope of a transformed, modern, socially relevant Church. It gave those on the fringes of faith hope of finding something to believe in. Even now it has the power to shock and provoke. Despite being derivative and hastily written, it remains fresh. I used it as a set text for second-year undergraduate theology students throughout the 1990s and was amazed at some of the responses. Those with no church backgrounds read the text and often remark: 'If I sensed from Christians and churches I know that they were wrestling with some of the issues found in *Honest to God*, then I'd be much more interested.'

The hopes were not dashed immediately, but they were certainly not fulfilled. In 1964, Mark Gibbs and Ralph Morton published *God's Frozen People: A book for – and about – ordinary Christians.*[7] Reading it now reveals the extent to which it has, inevitably, dated. It refers to 'the layman' in a cringe-worthy way. It fights battles (for women's ordination, for example) long won in most parts of

Christianity. But some of its insights remain disturbingly pertinent. They argue for the centrality of the laity in thinking about Christianity. They claim, in effect, the sad reality of the 'unfinished Reformation'. Until Christianity can see itself as helping people make sense of their ordinary lives via their faith, then it will not have begun to do its task. They note the shift away from the primacy of family and village life to different social units. Towns, cities and social mobility really have changed things about the way we think about our primary social groupings (in families and friendships, and at work). Thinking about faith has to adjust to these changes. They note the enormous impact of the expansion of leisure time and opportunities upon the structure of people's lives. And in this, and especially in their 1971 work *God's Lively People: Christians in Tomorrow's World* they begin to map out the educational challenges delivered to Christianity in the West by such changes as these.[8]

The disturbing aspect of a re-reading of Gibbs' and Morton's work is the enormity of the task adult educators have faced, and still do face, in encouraging British Christians to accept these changes, and the impact of them upon Christian faith. Bowden's pessimism is understandable because, nearly fifteen years later, he saw so little development. Twenty-five years further on, I want to be less pessimistic. The time for pessimism is long over. We are in crisis time, yes. But the cultural climate is different from Bowden's time. Precisely because spirituality is booming, and anti-religious hostility has been replaced by non-religious ignorance, there is a new educative task to be undertaken inside and outside churches.

But why is this a 'new Christian liberal' task? It has often been said that as soon as you give someone a theological education, you turn them into a liberal. I want to note in a positive way a sense in which this quip is true. You cannot educate someone without requiring them to be more open and attentive than they once were. In that sense, a liberalizing process is inevitable. But I don't want that insight to remain theoretical. In my teaching – especially of those training for various forms of church ministry, or in evening classes of those in the later stages of life who undertake theology 'for sheer interest' in their own (often very precious) spare time – the impact of theological education has often been staggering. Those of twenty or thirty years' adult Christian experience often become extremely angry that the type of things I introduce in biblical studies or in theology classes have made so few inroads into church life.

Theological education at its best demands an openness which does not seem required in much church life. 'Churchy' existence can cocoon people. Theological education can thus relate more to 'the world of work' or to the 'real life' in which most people spend their time. When done well, it helps people interpret life, not run away from it. Perhaps the reasons that many branches of Christianity have been so fearful of their 'young people' undertaking theological study is precisely because it has prepared them for real life and not simply for the Church.

It is not, however, true that theological education turns everyone into the same type of Christian. Of course, it can be argued that seminary/theological college/theological course training is more likely to 'school' people into particular confessions, or into denominational traditions. Critics could point to this being 'training' rather than 'education'. There may be some truth in this. Attention to 'practice' rather than 'theory', whilst understandable in order to oppose too cerebral and disconnected an approach to learning, has its limits.[9] But the necessary partnerships between theological colleges, courses and universities (providing co-teachers and functioning as validating bodies for awards) prevent, at their best, lazy distinctions being drawn between education and training, and between theory and practice. Furthermore, as we noted earlier, universities are not as free of values, in a safe haven of objectivity, as has been supposed.

Theological education on a mass scale, then, has to be a crucial part of Christianity's future in Britain. People inside churches need to know more about their faith, its history, how it works and what it can and cannot achieve. People on the fringes of churches and well beyond them need to have the chance to be well-informed about religions (and not just their buildings and artifacts, but also what they're for and how they work), and about Christianity as one of those religions.

In making such an assertion, and defining it as a proposal within a 'new Christian liberalism' I am, of course, opening up this revised, chastened liberalism to an old charge: this new liberalism is as élitist as the old. But it's worth taking the risk. Education need not be élitist. It is only so when not available, or not made accessible, to as many people as possible, and as many who want it. It has to risk trying to argue for its acceptance even by those who do not want it. But no one can be forced to be educated. And no one can predict the outcome of education (otherwise it would be brainwashing). That is why education is unreservedly liberal, and part of the creative work of God in the world today.

The new Christian liberalism will resist being allied with an 'anything goes' culture.

Our inability to predict what education might achieve and the acceptance that diversity in Christianity is irreducible do not, though, conspire together to support a view that 'anything goes'. Liberalism itself has always worked with clear commitments. Its weakness in the past was that it inadequately articulated the range of those commitments. Through an understandable desire to stress its capacity for openness and critique, it has been resistant to showing where its limits lay. Times have changed. There have to be theological equivalents to the limits more perceptible in the world of ethics. The challenge is simply to find out what these are, when the temptation is always to cut short the difficult explorations necessary.

An example from the world of ethics makes the point.[10] It is clear that Adolf Eichmann was wrong in the part he played in Nazism. No ethical position can be justified to support medical experimentation on healthy innocent human beings, simply on the basis of their ethnic origin. This insight might well be claimed to derive specifically from a post-Enlightenment, human rights, western liberal modernist perspective. But it also appears to be true. It cannot be claimed, without further analysis, both that Nazism is a product of (unifying, totalitarian-oriented) western post-Enlightenment thought and that the critique of Nazism is a similar product, and that both positions are equally true. Liberalism does not say that 'both are valid' (as the caricature of liberalism would have it). Liberalism notes that both exist (and only in this very limited sense are they 'valid') and requires that each be subject to critical scrutiny. Within that process of critical scrutiny, a way beyond indifference becomes clear.[11]

At root is a further western post-Enlightenment agenda item: a concern for human rights. This concern has never meant that anyone can do anything to anyone. It contains within it a recognition that constraints have to be defined, in order to foster human flourishing. The new dimension in thought which has led to a critique of some facets of western liberalism (understood here more in economic terms) is that despite the emergence of the human rights agenda in explicit political form from a western base, the flourishing of all has not always led, in the West, to the recognition that this may mean the self-imposed curtailment of the freedom of some. To use a simple economic argument: I should perhaps be made to be less free to purchase the cheap(-ish) computer on which I write, in the interests of the greater well-being of the distant (doubtless low-paid) employees who put it together.

A more far-fetched, but persuasive, theological example could also be offered. It might be deemed right to permit as 'valid' the view that God is an invisible red spider. Aside from the question of how one could ever know this (something which critics of religion offer as a charge to any belief in God), there are even more basic questions worth asking. Who follows this God? How does their belief have an impact on themselves and others? It may be concluded that such followers, whether they be many or few, should be left to continue in their belief, as it is 'harmless'.[12] Should such a belief be linked to an aggressive campaign of proselytization, then it would be a different matter. And even so, it would not take too much critical analysis to show that there might be better ways of conceiving God, drawing on more tried and tested traditions and practices.

That liberalism's enduring emphases have been release, freedom and openness on a number of fronts may, of course, have implied a boundless liberation. Theological liberalism, however, has always contained within it the desire and the resources necessary to offer a critique of 'anything goes' culture. Without succumbing to a lazy version of orthodoxy (for orthodoxies themselves must always be questioned), it has been aware of the danger of colluding with less desirable forms and expressions of liberalism (e.g., ethical and economic). It has perhaps been less sharp than it might have in seeing the danger of confusing what can be believed ('validity' in a weak sense) with what it is worth believing (validity on the way towards truth).

New forms of Christianity must be unreservedly 'secular'.

There are consequences from the six preceding discussion starters which are far-reaching. Christian liberalism accepts a complex and critical interaction with diverse versions of truth and reality, as it seeks to clarify who God is, what God is like, what Christianity is, and what Christianity distinctly offers to humankind's knowledge of God. This has always been an emphasis and strength of liberalism. It is not alone in having such an emphasis. Its uniqueness has resided in the courageous and consistent extent to which it has maintained it, often to its own cost. But we can now see how misleading it can be to speak in terms of 'secular Christianity', or to praise the 'secular' too simply. Christianity is not and cannot be secular. It is a religious movement and (complex set of) worldview(s) which begins from the conviction that God is, and affirms that God is as God is in Jesus Christ. Thereafter, it is willing to admit a struggle to define matters any further. It is, though, committed to search for further definition, and to do so explicitly in the context of the wider world. Only for that reason have liberalism and secularity been closely allied.

We have, though, noted the radically secular context within which religions do their work, and therefore how their primary contributions in British society are inevitably shaped. Christianity, as we have seen, needs to re-assert its role as a living religion in British society, aware that it is doing so in a highly secularized society. It is seeking to do this at a time when spirituality is on the increase. We can call this a 'spiritual age' if we so wish. This is not necessarily good news for religion. But it recognizes a potential receptivity for what Christianity has to say about God, human beings, and society, if Christianity can present itself appropriately. The secularity of British culture admittedly determines how religions have to present themselves. They have to argue a case for the viability of being 'religious' (as opposed to 'spiritual') at all. They must also show how such 'religiosity' is genuinely interpretative of, and informative for, the living of daily life. Unlike the 1960s and 1970s, when much of secular society was 'baptized' in the hope of people seeing Christianity's relevance, the contemporary approach must not be focused on relevance, but on viability. And it must accept the religiosity of Christianity, not try and pretend that it is otherwise. In this sense, the post-liberal reaction to liberalism has shown its worth. We are not to be afraid of 'church' any more. But we need to be prepared to acknowledge the limitations of churches as we know them. New communal forms of Christianity may yet be to come.

This is not a very clear argument.)

Secular encounters with God need religious communities to be known as such.

I opened this book with reference to the challenge that Jane Craske and I issued to readers of our 1999 co-edited book *Methodism and the Future*. What can we possibly say to our contemporaries to help them begin to appreciate what we see religion to be *for*? And how can we begin to do it when there seem so many other pressing (more interesting?) things with which they should fill their time. As the saying goes: 'the rubber hits the road' at this point. In the complex interface between religious and secular worlds/readings of society, what can we say that religion will achieve? This discussion starter expresses a possible answer: secular encounters with God need religious communities to be known as such. In other words, in the rich mix of life experiences, and within the vast variety of communal settings in which those experiences are had, there needs to be at least one community or set of communities in which a theological interpretation of human living is explicitly offered. Otherwise, people will have no obvious context, and no regular place, within which to interpret their lives in relation to a belief in God.

The deeper challenge though, of course, is then to clarify why a theological interpretation of life should be offered at all. Why is it necessary (or even useful) for life to be related to a belief in God? We could say: we need to relate life to God because God is there, is the source of all life, and so we are respecting the one who created all things. This may well be so. But critics might argue that though the world is, on the whole, a nice place, there is too little evidence of the creating God around to justify this claim. It is much less hassle to carry on as if there were no God. There seems no *need* to assume that God is. Gone, after all, are the days when we need to be afraid of God, now that we know that natural disasters and thunderbolts are not to be equated with divine judgements. If we are to speak of God as 'judge' at all, then we must do so more thoughtfully and more subtly. *The Judgment of God's terrible non-intervention (HB)*

At this point we cannot avoid facing the further question, therefore, of what God is like. If God is not to be feared in this way, then what's the point? The question 'What's the point?' turns everything, of course, into a rather self-serving, utilitarian kind of exercise. It implies that God's existence is dependent on whether or not God is useful for our life. I want to resist such pragmatism. Yet I also accept that this is the ground on which I must argue. I want finally to claim that God is 'useful' because God is, and is worth working at (as a concept) and living within (as a reality). But I accept the necessity to argue via usefulness. People need to be shown there will be some pay-off in all of this. Christianity is about salvation, after all, and that means something happens to people who believe. However, people believe God to be, and be like, many different things. For some, God remains a tyrant who controls, or at least monitors, their every move, curtailing their freedom. For others God is a warm, cosy grandfather figure who receives them into his arms regardless of what they've done without any word of advice, warning or reprimand. Whilst the latter is more attractive (and psychologically less harmful), it doesn't seem to be quite what Judaism and Christianity have been trying to get at in their talk of God. God as tyrant, however, is clearly not the only alternative.

So why interpret life with respect to God? It should be done because a life lived with reference to the traditions of God can produce a life far richer than one lived without such reference. A God held to be the source of all love and justice is not simply viewed as a set of principles by which one should seek to live. Such a God is also held to be the source of such power to live. A recognition of the necessity to live in awareness of such a God becomes an empowering awareness of human limitation, and not an excuse for not making one's own decisions or taking up one's own responsibility. And in the quest to clarify who God is, all the questions about ultimate values and principles are, in any case, encapsulated.

All of this does not, of course, mean that lives lived without God are inevitably unconcerned with love and justice. But awareness of God, or even a desire to use the 'God traditions' or the 'God stories' (i.e., the words which religions have come up with to talk about reality and its source), puts people on a particular track. It invites people to live in an 'ultimacy-conscious' way, rather than simply for the moment alone, for themselves alone, or even for their own kind. In terms of specific religions, it has then to be asked: but what does a particular claim that God is like x, y or z amount to?

Christians offer a range of answers. At their most basic Christian answers include: God is Trinity, or God is Christ-like. Both of these need further unpacking. But they can be seen as efforts to say the following. God is relational (as Trinity), and therefore profoundly concerned with all manner of relationships. God (as Christ-like) is deeply connected with the material world, and lives, in a sense, inside it. God suffers with it (in crucifixion), and yet is not consumed by its suffering, for, as the source of all life, God is always able to go on giving life to the world (resurrection).

Lives are thus, in Christian understanding, to be lived within such beliefs about God. And for such basic beliefs to be sustained there need to be people who keep on maintaining and reflecting upon such beliefs. The practice of churches, whatever else it is, must therefore be about the critical, creative continuation of such traditions, so that people's life experience can be interpreted in the light of the reality of God.

There is no such thing as Christianity for solitary believers.

It is said that three Christians, a Roman Catholic, a Baptist and a Methodist, arrived at the pearly gates of heaven, to be accosted by St Peter. 'And what have you brought with you?' Peter asked. 'I've brought my rosary', said the Roman Catholic. 'Very good', replied Peter, 'in you go. And what about you?' 'Well I've got my Bible with me,' the Baptist said. 'Fine, on your way.' The Methodist meanwhile lifted up the tea towel on top of the object she was carrying and smiled: 'And I've brought a casserole!'

The Methodist tradition is strong on the togetherness, the social aspect, of Christian living. As the joke successfully reminds us, though, any group which stresses the social aspect of Christianity can too easily create cosy groups more interested in gathering to feed each other, and doing little else.[13] But there is no doubt that Methodism is on to something. The 'corporate' or 'communal' character of Christian living is not just about the fact that there are lots of Christians who occasionally meet together. Religions usually (there are some exceptions) thrive on groups. People need to interact as part of their religious practice. This is how people access a religious tradition. You don't simply learn it as an individual. You 'inhabit' a set of practices, which you pick up by being part of a group. More than that, though, you are likely to be deeply shaped by the views of particular religious believers with whom you mix most frequently.[14] So the formation of those primary groups to which you belong is going to be a crucial question.

And yet those with whom you mix most often need to be able

I would not last / reminds a christian / without group life at / many levels.

both to sustain and to challenge you in your own religious beliefs. Without sustenance, the whole of life becomes a long set of unanswered questions with nothing firm to build upon. Without challenge, religion becomes avoidance of difficult questions, based on the assumption that what I believe is true (regardless of what anyone else thinks). Good religion will permit neither to be absent and will require the sustaining and challenging functions to occur within concrete communities. Unless people are linked with others and both upheld and provoked through their involvement with supportive others, good religion cannot result. Belonging and believing go inextricably together.

The notion of a 'networked' and 'networking' understanding of the Church has considerable value.

The importance of 'belonging', though, goes much further than this. To stress that one cannot be a solitary believer may imply that belonging to a local group of believers were enough. This, though, would be to underplay the global context within which, as we saw in Chapter 2, we now live. In an age dominated by language drawn from the use of computers, the notion of religions being global networks of local area networks is compelling. If religions do not aspire to be universal in scope, then they are being untrue to their intent to deal with truth claims (i.e., to be dealing with what really is, and what really matters, potentially for all people). This is both the strength and weakness of religions. Yet viewing religions as 'networks' also begins to respect of concreteness of the links that they make between people.

Christianity is thus itself best viewed as a network of networks: a global structure which brings together many groupings of local communities of Christians. To be at either extreme without respect for the opposite pole is to disrespect what Christianity is and how it works. In other words, to be local without respecting the global movement of which one is a part is to fail to respect Christianity as a religion, that is, that it is in the ultimacy business. To be global, without respecting the complex diversity of settings within which the concretely local forms of Christianity take shape is to disrespect both Christianity's own form of materialism (incarnation), and the fact that religions are about living.

The way that religions work in the contemporary, pluralist world has potential political spin-offs, if only we could see this. Religions are universal structures with very local forms. They compete with each other, in effect, at every level, even whilst interweaving with each other in many and complex ways, across the world. They make truth claims in what they say and in how they function. Despite the frequent absoluteness of their claims and structures, they are required to recognize their relativity through the other traditions alongside which they co-exist. And in the case of each religion, structures exist which require of individual believers that they look beyond themselves and their own, limited world.

In Britain, it is possible through their participation in Christianity for people:

- to belong consciously to a global organization;
- to be aware of their locality;
- to ask ultimate questions about themselves, their immediate society and the world;
- to be conscious of participating within a complex political structure (the Church);
- to work at what it means to be a political animal;
- to recognize the ideological diversity of their involvement (there are other churches and other religions);
- to explore how their participation relates to their more explicit 'political' commitments.

Being Christian in Britain can thus be seen, helpfully, as a major political act, if only we would see it as such.

'Virtual communities' are not enough.

The language of 'networks' comes from the world of computers. The computer world has also supplied the phrase 'virtual community'. Christianity can be thought of as a 'virtual community' both as a historical phenomenon (the Church throughout the centuries, with members both living and long dead), and as a contemporary, global reality (the Church throughout the world). In this respect the phrase 'virtual community' is useful. It is useful too with respect to the 'actual' virtual communities which have brought Christians around the world, and in local 'groups', together via their screens and monitors. Such virtual communities have, for example, kept people frustrated with local churches in touch with Christianity, have provided solace for searchers, and created 'churches' for those of limited physical mobility.

The phrase 'virtual community' is, however, insufficient as a term for Christianity's grasp on what it means to be a Christian alongside others. For computer-generated understandings of virtual communities sit too easily with the avoidance of implications of embodiment. The denial of our materiality, our inherent corporateness (understood both as embodiment, and togetherness), coheres too readily with an individualism which prioritizes the solitary mind. Despite all the supposed materialism of the contemporary age, it is a profound danger of a screen-oriented culture.

Religious believers remain individual human beings, however important the emphases upon the social dimensions of religious belief undoubtedly are.

The tenor of so much of this and previous chapters has been to stress the irreducibly social dimensions of religious belief, and thus of being Christian. This has resulted from the recognition on many fronts of the way that religions work. It has also come from the realization that a damaging kind of individualism has to be opposed, both in religion and society. Having said all this, the history of Christianity offers too many nagging reminders (and liberalism is one of these) of the importance of individuals in their attitude towards God, for the social dimension of religion to get out of hand. Indeed, this is not just an issue for religion, as psychologist Anthony Storr wrote in 1988:

> The current emphasis upon intimate personal relationships as the touchstone of health and happiness is a comparatively recent phenomenon. Earlier generations would not have rated human relationships so highly; believing, perhaps, that the daily round, the common task, should furnish all we need to ask; or, alternatively, being too preoccupied with merely keeping alive and earning a living to have much time to devote to the subtleties of personal relations.[15]

It could be claimed, then, that an emphasis upon the social dimensions of religion merely serves some deeper cultural shift.

There is undoubtedly a strong current in contemporary thinking away from individualism. This is, in my view, an appropriate shift. Storr's quotation does, however, put that shift in context. The individualism of (liberal) modernity is to be opposed not by a return to some lost golden (perhaps medieval) age. A better social form of Christianity did not exist back then. Christianity was different, and better in some respects, perhaps, but not all. And there are dangers attached to potentially submerging the individual in a socially understood religion. Opposition to a damaging individualism could lead to a loss of the reminder that people still need to commit themselves as individuals to something rather than nothing. There is an individuality appropriate to all religious belief, one which respects the individual pole of what it means to be human. One is never only solitary and never only social as a human being. One is always both.

But Storr's quotation contains a further useful insight. In speaking of 'intimate personal relationships' he is referring to a particular aspect of the contemporary emphasis upon the communal, the social, the relational. We are dealing here with a particular type and quality of human relating. Perhaps this is the context within which the future of religions, and thus of Christianity in Britain, is best discussed. The individualism of the past can be viewed as 'something bad'. It can also be seen, as Storr reminds us, as a fight for survival. In the West we are on a daily basis all too insufficiently aware of how many around the world, and in our own communities, continue this fight for survival. But at the same time, in the material comfort which many western citizens enjoy (though through the sweat of many within and beyond the West), we have glimpsed what is possible beyond the question of survival. Concern for 'intimate personal relations' reflects this comfort. It is also an acknowledgement that attention to the fullest human living must always look both at how one lives as an individual, and how one lives in relation to others. If religions do not contribute deeply to this debate then they really have lost their souls.

*   *   *

This chapter has built directly on the contentions of the previous two. The clarification of the religious context (Chapter 2) was followed by an exploration of the options from Christian theology and practice upon which any contemporary re-assertion of Christianity needs to take place (Chapter 3). In this chapter I have made a particular case for the contemporary usefulness of a chastened Christian liberalism. Such an approach to contemporary Christianity maintains its recognition that individuals have to work out what to commit themselves to. Individuals remain important. There is no such thing as vicarious belief,[16] and everyone has some beliefs (whether they choose to recognize them or not). But working out our commitments does not mean that we simply invent them. Traditions exist before we do, even if we shape them collectively through experience.

Nor is it a matter of indifference what people commit themselves to. Traditions and commitments are bound up with morals. Morals carry metaphysical implications. Furthermore, because there is no dodging embodiment (people have/are bodies) and conflict (embodied people disagree about what matters), then communities, not just individuals, are important too. It is communities which carry traditions. A Christian liberal future will thus be post-liberal and be stronger in its explicit recognition of the importance of the communal dimension of faith. But this post-liberal liberalism will maintain some clear liberal concerns from the past: to education, openness and criticism.

If this chapter has, however, supported a 'liberal' agenda, what has happened to the 'Protestantism' of the Liberal Protestant tradition into which this current work undoubtedly falls? It is to this that we must turn in the next chapter.

5

How to be a Protesting Christian without being Anti-Catholic

In Chapter 3 I suggested that denominationalism has not had its day, but that it is not the best way of handling Christian difference in the present. It may, then, seem strange that I should want to try and tease out the possible meanings of 'Protestantism' in looking to stimulate a positive and creative future for Christianity in Britain. That is, however, precisely what I shall do in this chapter. The arguments to be presented are very simple, and are all highly contentious. But they cry out for respect, given how easily Protestantism comes to be misunderstood, distorted (even by Protestants themselves) and thus devalued in western culture.

Protestantism is not a denomination.

Protestantism is not itself a denomination. It is a collective term for a whole set of movements (and eventually denominations) in Christianity which sprang up in the wake of the early-sixteenth-century Reformers' critiques of the Church in western Europe, then centred on Rome. As a term, the word 'Protestant' was first used in 1529 of the German Lutheran princes who protested against the freedom of a state to determine its own religious allegiance.[1] There were, however, never any 'Protestants' of a single confession, as Protestants by definition protested in different ways, using different confessions of faith, against imposition of a particular form of Christian faith as decreed by the Church in Rome.

In its origins lie both Protestantism's strength and its weakness. Its strength lies in its insistence that the grounds need to be clarified upon which one's faith is based. Appeal to the Church alone would not be adequate in future. How were the Scriptures being used?

What place was there for the grace of God? How did Christ fit in? Its weakness lies in the seeds of fragmentation which the early years planted. With hindsight it may be possible to argue that, despite the constant message throughout Protestantism's history that the various resulting denominations were Christians continuous with historic Christianity, insufficient checks were built into the protest to show how and why such divergence should or should not lead to institutional separation. But that's with hindsight. Whatever the structural and political consequences of the sixteenth-century 'protests', Protestantism may perhaps best now be understood as a mood or style of Christianity, which, like Pentecostalism, needs constantly to irrupt at particular times within Christian history to keep Christianity on course.

We need not all be Protestants now, but a form of post-modern Protestantism would be a welcome development in British Christianity.

I am not, then, arguing for a mass conversion of Roman Catholics to a Protestant denomination. Nor am I suggesting that all Protestants veer towards a particular confession within Protestantism. I am asking what the Protestant mood or style of Christianity has to contribute to contemporary thinking about the future of Christianity in Britain. British Christianity, I contend, needs to be a form of post-modern Protestantism. The main contours of this, as far as the modernity/post-modernity debate is concerned, have already been sketched in the previous two chapters, via the debate between liberalism and post-liberalism. Here I must simply add why a re-assertion of a form of Protestantism is so necessary at the moment. In making this claim, I am disagreeing with Kenneth Leech, whose writings I otherwise usually find both accurate in their analysis and helpful in the suggestions they make. Writing in 1992 Leech states:

> The only hope for a Christian response to the contradictions and dilemmas of contemporary capitalism lies in a renewed Catholicism which is able to engage with the structures of advanced technological society.[2]

Leech is, of course, taking full account of the emphases of many of the movements I sketched in Chapter 3. He recognizes the power of liturgy and the need to recover a sense of its importance. He is strong on the communal dimension of Christianity, and savage in his criticism of individualism. He also demonstrates many of the positive facets of the new Christian liberalism I sought to espouse in Chapter 4 (critical dialogue, openness, and education). My dispute with Leech is simply as to why Catholicism should be the logical contemporary framework within which to re-discover and promote fresh interest in Christianity today. I do not dispute that it is one channel. (In saying this I am a quintessential liberal! Let many flowers bloom.) But evangelicals must have their say too, as must Orthodox and charismatic Christians. My own apologia for a revised, chastened Liberal Protestantism is simply because of the critical, intellectually challenging edge which this tradition has traditionally brought to its promotion of Christianity. At its best this would, in fact, cohere well with so much of what Leech himself espouses. As I have stressed, liberalism is caricatured when seen as a weak, 'anything goes' kind of Christianity. Leech himself is a protesting Anglo-Catholic. In so being, he is the best form of Liberal Protestant, whether he would care to admit it or not.

Some of the best Protestants are Roman Catholics.

This comment upon Kenneth Leech and his work leads neatly into the next point. Not only can an Anglo-Catholic be a good Liberal Protestant. Roman Catholics can be good protesting Christians too. The late Adrian Hastings is a good example of a prominent critical Roman Catholic. In the past thirty years or so, Hans Küng, Edward Schillebeeckx, Leonardo Boff and Tissa Balasuriya have all made the headlines due to their falling out of favour with the Vatican. The danger of such publicity, of course, is that it merely highlights the fact that 'protesting' seems only ever to be about protesting against an out-of-date church. Protestants can look on and use the way that such thinkers are treated as further proof of how out of touch, or just plain wrong, the Roman Catholic Church is.

There is undoubtedly continuity here between the origins of Protestantism in the strict historical sense of the term, and the internal debates of contemporary Roman Catholicism. But I make this observation merely to extend the point that Protestantism is best understood less as a confession (and certainly not as a denomination), and more as a style of Christianity which any Christian can adopt. Some of the best protestors are Roman Catholic not because they are criticizing the church, or making the headlines, but because they recognize in their understanding of Christianity, and in the exercise of a life of faith, that there is a strong element of 'protest' at its heart, and embody it in their practice. It is far from accidental that liberation theology in its Latin American forms was cultivated heavily in Roman Catholic soil.

Protestantism seeks to put God first.

But what does Protestantism actually stand for? A number of summaries of Protestantism's main tenets have been offered over the years.[3] In the discussion starters to follow I offer just one possible reading. *Who verges it at first – the heart of Calvinism*

The first tenet is that Protestantism seeks to put God first. This sounds a deeply pious intent and is often used in a far too 'holier than thou' form than is good for its users. For it can mean '*we* put God first, and *others* don't', when it is more accurate (and, in fact, more true to Protestant sensibility) to note that all Christians may seek to put God first, but that all fail. But it remains an important starting-point, because this re-assertion of the priority of God in Christian faith and life is where it all began for Protestantism in the post-Reformation period.

There are negative aspects to the tenet. Putting God first entails not putting the Church first, and not putting the state first. It even means not putting the Bible first, despite the emphasis that all Protestants would be expected to attach to the Scriptures. Expressed positively, it entails recognizing that all life is from God, and that all well-being (salvation, redemption) and any hope for the world are to be found in God alone. There is an implicit criticism in attaching too much significance to human thought, action and aspiration. Human beings are put firmly in their (limited) place.

These positive and negative aspects to this 'priority of God' tenet, however, need further glossing. For the history of Protestantism requires us to qualify any claim that Protestants have somehow got this more right than others. In actual practice, in seeking to put God first, Protestants have often ended up putting their own personal

agenda, their own kind (nation, people) or their own sect first. They
have ended up putting human experience first (their human experience of God), and thus have sometimes seemed to talk more of their
own faith, than of God. They have thus ended up 'believing in themselves' more than in the God in whom their self-belief supposedly
resides. And at its most extreme, this self-belief has seemed to be a
belief in self and nothing more, an ultimate atomism based around a
conviction that Protestantism frees you to believe as an individual.
For Protestantism does indeed free you to believe as an individual.
But, as I have stressed throughout, this was never meant to mean
that you could simply decide in isolation what it is worth believing
in.

In critiquing the distortions of this first tenet, we are back with its
positive aspect. The priority of God means being released from all
forms of complete self-reliance. Putting God first means recognizing that God always was and is independent of all (necessary)
human attempts to grasp something of the reality of God (in words,
pictures, music or whatever). That independence of God frees
human beings from having to invent God, however creative we must
be in our grasping after God, and however understandable it may be
that we try and achieve things on our own. We clearly carry huge
responsibility in the world. But the claim that this is a God-given
responsibility both clarifies our limits, and indicates where we must
look for help in deciding how to act.

Protestantism is unreservedly critical.

Protestantism was, though, born in criticism. Even if it must always
ensure that it moves beyond debilitating anti-Catholicism, there is
no escaping its critical edge. In order to maintain its first tenet – putting God first – it will have to remain true to its second: constant
criticism. These first two tenets belong inextricably together. It is an
arrogant claim, for how do we know we are being appropriately
critical, from a justifiable base? But in order to be consistent,
Protestants have to be aware that the tenet can be turned against
Protestantism itself. As Dillenberger and Welch put it:

> Against every such claim to absoluteness (whether religious or
> social and political) Protestantism must protest. Every religious

institution, every creed, every pattern of worship, shares in the limitations and distortions (i.e., sin) of human existence. No religious pattern or form can be exempt from criticism in the light of fresh appropriation of the truth.[4]

It is easy to see how such a principle could lead to institutional fragmentation. More and more groups would soon begin to claim that they, and they alone, had freshly appropriated the truth. In doing so, though, they had failed to apply the principle to their own group. It is also easy to note the irony of how such a principle could lead beyond modernism into the more relativistic form of post-modernism, in which the desire to oppose the absoluteness of any human idea or institution has become so all-pervasive that no criticism is possible. At such a point, the Protestant Principle has caused the Reformation to eat its own tail.

Neither of these poles is the true heir to the Reformation, and the true legacy of the sixteenth-century protest which gave confessional Protestants their name. The critical principle of genuine Protestantism is the requirement that any and every Christian movement go on asking of itself how, as it proceeds in good faith, it is putting God first.

Protestantism feeds the independent spirit.

Being born of such criticism, however, Protestants often become independent. As a style of Christianity, further, it appeals to people of independent personality type. This is tricky territory which cannot be gone into fully here. Some observations must, though, be ventured.

On the one hand, it might have to be accepted that this style of Christianity is not for all. Despite the claim that Christianity contains an irreducible prophetic dimension, not all are prophets. Not all Christians seem cut out for a life on the edge (of Church, or society). On the other hand, the recognition that the Protestant style of Christianity feeds the independent spirit can suggest that you have to be a maverick, an outsider, in order to be Christian. Indeed, you prove your faith by your awkwardness. Again, neither pole fully and successfully captures what the independent streak within Protestantism ought to amount to. But there can be no denying its existence. Constant critique, in order to attempt to put God first, can lead to conflict. It is not a comfortable style of Christianity. But equally it demands of Protestants more than they have often been willing to admit of the reasons why, collectively and individually, they should ever go it alone.

The psychological impact of this aspect of Protestantism should not, however, be underestimated, and can be illustrated through many examples. When I was a student I lived in a hall of residence in which there lived a Christian who felt that he was not being a true witness unless he was proving unpopular with the student body. If ever he became socially 'accepted' therefore, he felt he was becoming worldly and would distance himself from people. Even if this could be argued to be psychological imbalance, and nothing to do with religion, this is not how he saw it, and not how he presented himself. It would be wrong, in my view, to deny this tendency within Protestantism.

If this early concrete example of this tendency proved fruitful for me, I can illustrate it yet further through more recent experience of my own. I am typing this text in a Southern state of the USA. For the first time, I am in the USA not as a student, tourist, or conference attender. It has provided me with the opportunity to get inside a different 'mindset' for a while, in a context starkly different from that out of which I am essentially writing. Unlike my British, Yorkshire setting, where it seems unusual and freakish to own up to any kind of religion, in the South of the USA it is unusual not to be Christian. As it is only half-jokingly said:

> Being Southern is thinking of church as a habit, like putting on shoes or setting your clock; humming hymns while you wash your dog; knowing when to shout 'Amen!' 'Hallelujah!' or 'Yes, Brother!' at meetings; and talking about Jesus like he grew up next door.[5]

Christianity is thus not unusual (everyone has to be some type of Christian or other) and seems profoundly conformist. It is, however, allied directly with a deep-rooted independence of spirit, related to American history. 'We are rebels down here', I was told, even though the speaker seemed to be materially comfortable and politically and theologically conservative. But the rebelliousness is not merely a historical sense of having opposed the Northern 'Yankees' in the Civil War. A direct link is assumed to exist between the Protestantism and the sense of independence. As I have sought to show throughout this book, it is more than half true. But it is also, dangerously, half untrue too.

I mention the context of writing for a personal reason. A famous North Carolina resident was deeply influential upon the Christian context in which I grew up. Billy Graham came from Charlotte, North Carolina, to lead many 'evangelistic crusades' in Britain in the 1950s and 1960s. He influenced my parents, and many of those who shaped my formative understanding of Christianity. The songs and hymns he used (many much older than Graham himself) were made popular in a variety of songbooks and their use spread throughout British Christianity during the 1960s and 70s. For those of us within that world (and it has become clear to me that there are more than care to admit it!), the 1960s and 70s were not decades of flower-power and permissiveness, but of buoyant evangelical Christianity. British post-war optimism and emergent prosperity linked with Southern-state religion to produce a powerful religious movement with clear undercurrents which were at once social, political and psychological. Encountering Southern-states evangelicalism even now, I hear echoes of my youth. I encounter, too, a context for Christianity which many now in influential positions in churches in Britain – in many different denominations – simply wish continued to exist. For all the strengths of that form of evangelicalism it is ultimately ill-equipped to handle adequately pluralism, secularization's complexity, and intellectual rigour in Christianity. It is too prone to latch on to a form of political conservatism which relates the notion of independence to an individualistic version of Christian faith.

These examples show that the independent spirit is neither as simple as it may at first seem, nor always as positive. It can remain a close ally of the critical edge which Protestantism promotes and must be preserved. But it needs treating with some caution.

Protestantism is Christocentric.

Protestantism is Christocentric. Protestants make Jesus Christ central not as a rival to God (Christocentrism is not an alternative to Theocentrism), but as the crucial expression of what the God who they deem to be central in Christianity is like.[6] They have not, in other words, spent a lot of their time in reflecting on the doctrine of the Trinity, even though that doctrine forms the bedrock upon which all thinking about Christ has occurred. They frequently do their God-talk, therefore, directly in the form of reflection upon the figure of that independent spirit, Jesus of Nazareth. If you are trying to be an awkward so-and-so, then Jesus of Nazareth seems to be a good role model. Christocentrism and the critical spirit of Protestantism thus readily converge.[7]

Calvin's Institutes are about the Trinity basically!

Christocentrism does not simply mean 'putting Jesus first'.

'Christocentrism' does, though, need a bit more unpacking. Reduce the centrality of Jesus Christ to a few memories of his prophetic acts (trotting into Jerusalem on a donkey, for example, or throwing over the money-changers' tables), and things become somewhat distorted. Treat him as a teacher alone and before you know where you are, you've reduced Jesus Christ to *the teaching of Jesus of Nazareth* (as a set of ideas and principles, or a batch of good stories), and the figure himself is dispensable. So Christocentrism doesn't simply mean putting Jesus first. It means more than this. Christocentrism includes respecting the teaching of Jesus, and includes respect for his actions. It also means trying to get one's head around what resurrection means, what being a follower of Jesus Christ entails, and what both of those imply for human existence today. Let me take each in turn.

Let me be clear: I haven't got a clue what happened after Jesus' death. I don't know where Jesus' body went: whether it really was put in a tomb, whether it rotted like the rest of those who were crucified (or was eaten by dogs), or whether it was miraculously transformed so that Jesus re-appeared exactly as the Gospels describe. I am aware that the Gospels finish with some baffling texts, which don't speak with unanimity about the nature of Jesus' body. I know that in all ensuing Christian discussion, resuscitation (of Jesus' corpse), resurrection and immortality have been regularly confused. I note that many contemporary Christians, when they speak of resurrection, are primarily referring to the immortality of the spirit. I know, too, that the Apostle Paul (and the Christian Church after him) has also spoken of the resurrected body of Christ in a different way, to refer to people (the Church as the body of Christ).

But I believe in the resurrection of Jesus Christ. This means that participation in what Jesus stood for and in the same kind of life that he lived not only commits us to a particular way of living, but brings us into the sphere of spiritual power in which he himself participated. This was none other than the spirit of God. It is a spirit which cannot die. As long as there is life, there is God (and vice versa). The death of Jesus could not, then, possibly signify the end of God. Christian convictions about the raising of Jesus, then, are ways of pinpointing the particular action and presence of God in human history within the life of a specific individual and his surrounding context. Reference to the broader context (and on those who surround Jesus) is important. As feminist theologians have rightly stressed, it is not the solitary Jesus who constitutes the revelation of God, but Jesus in the company of others (disciples, followers, the healed, even sometimes the crowds). Christocentrism as an emphasis upon resurrection, then, means the constant availability of the life-giving God, in the context of life-giving human community.

Second, Christocentrism entails what is also often called 'discipleship'. For the figure of Jesus Christ to be truly central to one's life means following the way of Christ. This is not, as I have said, to be reduced to following a set of teachings. It includes giving attention to the teachings of Jesus of Nazareth, as found incorporated and interpreted within the Gospels of the New Testament. But it is more than this. Following a way will entail moving beyond, in the same spirit. It will mean dreaming dreams and taking actions of which Jesus of Nazareth could not have conceived. Yet working out 'in Christ' what these dreams and actions should be will need to be included within the act of following. The 'working out' will at least include argument with Christians and others, worship and prayer, theological reflection, political protest, and thoughtful ethical conduct.

Third, Christocentrism entails discovering how life is to be lived in the light of resurrection and discipleship. Life is to be lived constantly 'in Christ'. Yet 'in Christ' is to be understood neither individualistically nor ecclesiocentrically. Christocentrism is neither merely the goal of individual practice, nor to be subsumed within the assumption that the Church is everything. If Christocentrism means being focused upon the rule (or reign, or 'kingdom') of God, then this will include individual and church reflection and action. But determining what the rule of God (in Christ) means will go beyond these realms alone, and entail our clarifying how all our relationships, commitments and actions are to be interpreted in continuity with Jesus and in the light of attention to the presence of God in the world.

If Christocentrism means 'putting Jesus first', then it needs careful expansion. It is in my view better not to speak in such terms at all. Talking of Christian faith as 'putting Jesus first' seriously distorts what Christianity is and how it works. The centrality of Christ in Christian thought and practice, a crucial emphasis in Protestantism, requires a richer treatment than it often receives.

There is a sample of a 'Jesus religion' which I think he would have (characterised).

Protesting Christians can be lay or ordained.

One of the saddest aspects of the history of Protestantism is that a movement which challenged the clerical dominance of Christianity should end up contributing to the undermining of Christianity altogether. The secularization of the modern West is undoubtedly fed by the nature of Luther's challenge to Roman Catholicism. Luther, though, would now be appalled at what ensuing history has made of that challenge. He would not have expected people to have given up religion altogether, but to relate to it differently.

Christians who want to assert the importance of the laity look to Jesus at this point too, though. In some ways it could be regarded as a further aspect of Christocentrism! Jesus was not a cleric. Debates will remain as to how schooled he was officially in the Jewish religion, or to what extent he simply picked up the formal aspects of his religion on the hoof. But he was no priest in the official sense of the term. He is thus an excellent role model for a protesting Christian wishing to have a go at clergy.

He couldn't be!

These introductory comments form a framework within which what we may call the 'social status' of the contemporary religious person can be discussed. The role of the clergy has changed drastically in Britain in the last fifty years. Dovetailing with the rise in scale and standing of many other 'helping professions' (health care, counselling, social work), the decline of the clergy in both numbers and social status has been marked. My wife is regularly asked to authenticate people's passport photographs, one of the few areas of

This was very hard a (am phenomenoist opinion of Russell)

life where the authority of a 'minister of religion' still lingers. More often than not, though, outside of the church people have little knowledge of or special respect for ministers of religion. Moving into Rotherham four years ago, I was stunned to discover a parent of one of our son's friends expressing reservations about letting her son accompany ours to a church youth club, given 'what you read in the papers about clergy being paedophiles, and all that'. There is, then, some revisionary work worth doing here. It is an alarming sign when ministers of religion end up with such a low social status.

Even so, the fact remains that most 'religious' people are lay. We've now had five hundred years working on this one, and don't seem to have made too much headway. And lay people are going to become more and more significant in the leadership of the Church, both because of the way in which the social and political structure of British life has developed in the last century or so, and because churches have recognized that they can no longer devote so many resources directly to clergy training and support. Whether ordained or lay, however, Christians in Britain in the future will need to be even clearer about how their faith relates to, and interprets, ordinary human living. Religion may well become more prominent as spirituality continues to be fashionable. But ghettoized religion will not necessarily help people live daily life. Christianity will only be of significant use to its members and to British society when all of its participants, clergy and lay, work at the interface between church and society. In this context, it could be argued that a leaner, fitter body of clergy, with a more defined (if more limited, religious) role, and greater clarity as to how they support lay people in the world, is what is needed for the churches of tomorrow.[8]

Protestantism promotes individuality and freedom, but remains committed to the creation of Christian community and a civil society.

Sociologist Steve Bruce expresses well the Protestant contribution to individualism:

> The Reformation hastened the rise of individualism and of rationality, and both of these were fundamentally to change the nature of religion and its place in the world. Individualism threatened the communal basis of religious belief and behaviour, while

rationality removed many of the purposes of religion and rendered many of its beliefs implausible.[9]

This feeding of the independent spirit, and fostering of human freedom are decisive in Protestantism, as I have accepted throughout this book. I have, however, also sought to include reminders of the ways in which support for individualism must be qualified. At this point, the Liberal Protestant version of Christianity needs to remind itself of the ways in which – in both its liberalism and its Protestantism – it has always carried with it a counter-tendency to its apparent support for unchecked individualism.

The freedom of the independent spirit is supported: yes. But this does not mean that one can believe what one wants. Orthodoxies must be rigorously questioned and re-worked. They are not, however, valueless. On the contrary, they are necessary. Institutional structures are all fallible, limited, and run by sinful human beings. Diversity in structure and style of Christianity may well be needed. But the proliferation of denominations cannot be limitless if the same God is being worshipped by Christians throughout the world.

The same argument applies to political life. Diversity in structure and style of government may well be needed. But not all political systems are necessarily good and conducive to the fostering of human freedom and justice. The apparent alliance between liberal modernity and capitalism itself needs loosening at this point to demonstrate that western Christianity itself does not merely serve one political master. But Christianity's concern to work for a civil society remains clear. Such a civil society is one which works for the freedom of all rather than the few, but does not support an unrealistic (ultimately impossible) limitless freedom in which anyone can do anything. Christians will contribute to discussions as to what restraints are necessary in order to preserve the maximum freedom possible.

Any claim, then, that the logic of Protestantism may be deemed sociologically unrealistic, whilst understandable, is ultimately not to be sustained.

Protestantism is attractive to protestors.

Protest will thus happen in the context of the preservation of freedom. But it is right to ask constantly whose freedom is being protected. Protestantism was born historically in the context of the preservation of the religious freedom of those who did not want to accept the particular religion required of them. There is a logical alliance between that primary quest for freedom and others, for example, for political freedom, or for freedom of sexual expression. It is thus not surprising that protesting Christians can find (and have found) themselves working alongside liberation movements of all kinds.

Freedom is, though, always a freedom *from* and a freedom *for*. Despite the fact that different ways of believing may be possible within the Church of England itself, freedom from the Church of England meant freedom to believe differently, but still Christianly, in a Presbyterian, Congregational or Baptist way. Freedom from slavery meant release from an unjust system of work towards ownership of land and property and the right to receive a just reward for labour. Freedom from religious oppression means release from the imposition of any particular religion, with the right to practise any religion. Freedom from sexual oppression means release from the assumption that all people are heterosexual and must express their sexuality in a particular way within heterosexual marriage, towards the recognition that sexual expression is diverse. None of these 'freedoms for' implies a limitless, value-free range of options, however. Not all who claim to be Christian may actually be so. Not every exercise of the right of property ownership and work may be good. Not every religion works in the best interests of its members and the wider world. Not every expression of sexuality, inside or outside of marriage, may actually be conducive to human well-being. Few, though, would dispute the long-term significance of protest, and the necessity of protest in the expansion and preservation of appropriate freedoms.

It is ironic that the development of freedom movements in the West have often seemed to lead to the necessity to be free from the Church, when it is out of Christianity that so many of the currents of thought stimulating liberative activity have derived. And at the present time, we find ourselves at a juncture in western culture where the freedoms won – enshrined quintessentially, perhaps, in the United Nations Declaration of Human Rights – are under question because of the recognized need to curb the excessive freedoms which oppress others, whilst preserving the freedoms of some. The quest for civil society entails maintaining appropriate protest (questioning, argument) within the political process.

If there is to be a theological contribution to the expansion of such appropriate freedom, in the context of appropriate protest, then it is impossible for theology to be anything but political. Protesting Christians will always be equally aware of this dimension to Christianity. Protesting Christians who value theology will also be aware that the political implications of Christianity, whilst they must include political action, will not be exhausted by such action. Christians are contemplative (or reflective) activists, and not merely activists. But given both Protestantism's history, and the potential for theological traditions to function as critical conversation partners with any political structure or ethical mindset, Christianity in protesting mode should appeal readily to protestors in the present. At the very least, Christianity can ask of any protestors: By what theology (or philosophy, or ideology) are you thinking and acting?

Protestantism should especially appeal to oppressed groups.

A number of features of protesting Christianity come together in respect of socially oppressed groups. Protestantism was born as a freedom movement, and it has supported claims for rights of individuals and particular groups. Strange as it may seem now, from the perspective of WASPs in the affluent West,[10] Protestantism's style of Christianity sits more easily with the socially excluded, the misfits, the uncomfortable and the incomers. It is surprising that protesting Christianity has not consistently done more to draw on this aspect of its own history.

And yet this 'oppression strand' of Protestantism is deeply ingrained within it, and can be taken in two markedly different directions, one positive, the other negative. In its positive form it has supported particular ethnic churches (e.g., German Lutheran, African Methodist Episcopal), and class-conscious Christian movements (e.g., both Wesleyan and Primitive Methodism, early forms of Black Majority Churches). These movements have enabled Christianity to be shaped in a way conducive to the expansion of its reach to people for whom the then mainstream forms were inadequate.[11] In negative form, of course, such particularity supports a dangerous tribalism, or tends towards the individualism which has been such a feature of this book.

I can, however, bear witness in my own life experience to the sociological and psychological complexity of Protestantism at this point. There is little doubt that I was introduced in my youth to a fusion of working-class culture and conservative evangelicalism which fostered in me a sense of 'take no crap from anyone'. My Christianity by definition was to be of a protesting kind. It has, however, taken me years to disentangle some other features of this Christianity. For politeness was to accompany the prophecy. Being 'a good Christian' and politically conservative, I belonged to the 'aspiring' working class. I had to live out the mixed messages I received: be subservient and kind to the middle and upper classes (whilst aspiring to belong to them), yet protest at every point.

The disentangling process has, of course, been long and useful, as well as painful at times. A certain kind of theology is inevitably likely to accompany a protesting kind of Christianity. It is strong on God's judgement, human fallibility, and on salvation. But there are positive dimensions to the theology too. It gives everyone a role in God's plan (see the next discussion starter) and contains genuine hope – wherever and in whatever form that hope is held to come to fruition.

I have, though, never been able to find an adequate form of a theology of politeness. I don't think it's possible. I have, however, drunk deep of the theology of grace. God clearly speaks to and through a whole range of people, even those who are quite unlike me, and those I don't like. That is (one version of) grace. But it has still not evolved into a theology of politeness. Whether it is due to the dominance of the protesting form of Christianity with which I began, psychological blockage, or plain pig-headedness, I may never know, but there is something about Christianity in protesting mode which resists turning people into 'good Christians' in the socially acceptable sense in which the term is often used.

Christianity in the present should be able to capitalize on this feature of its life. It can support the weak and the lonely. It can challenge the comfortable. This is a crucial aspect of what Christianity is and does, and is a main dimension of Protestantism – or should be.

Protestantism incorporates a theology of 'somebodiness'.

Beyond the danger of tribalism, and in the support of the oppressed, Christianity contains a theology of 'somebodiness'.[12] Historically, Protestantism has fostered this sense that people have worth, even

' Nobodies'
became
'somebodies' — Jack Lawson
on Methodism.

when churches of particular times may not have echoed this funda-mental verdict of God upon creation. In group and in individual terms, this sense of worth has been decisive in lifting the lowly, and in countering social exclusion. It has, of course, been argued with some justification that Protestantism has not always carried through this theology as fully as it might have, into social and political realms. In spiritualizing the sense of worth felt by people, it some-times colluded with social and political structures which conspired to keep people in their (poor) place.

Furthermore, in late modernity, this dimension of Christianity leaves lingering traces throughout secularized western culture in rather less positive forms. Listen to an interview with most success-ful western pop singers, and at some point in the interview, when asked what they would say to aspiring young musicians, the com-ment will almost invariably be made: 'You can be whatever you want to be. If you really want something badly enough, then you can have it.' Similarly, sportspeople speak frequently of 'needing to believe in themselves' more in order to achieve great things.

There are important links here with Protestantism's cultivation of an appropriate self-belief. Yet distortions have clearly crept in as the theological notion at the root of this sense of human self-worth has evolved in relation to the therapeutic culture of late modernity. There is a difference between saying 'If you really, really want some-thing, you can go out and get it' and 'you are not likely to get what you really want unless you work for it'. The former lacks realism and feeds off the notion that the construction of the self lies wholly in the control of an individual. It denies an appropriate sense of interdependency at the heart of the human person which a funda-mental belief in the createdness of all things can provide. Again, 'belief in oneself' is helpful when signifying realistic self-knowledge and confidence in one's own known abilities. It is nothing short of self-deception if self-knowledge is misplaced.

But there can be little doubt that these ever-present features of the understanding of the self to be found in contemporary popular culture trade off dimensions of theological thinking that have been strongly encouraged within Protestantism. The challenge for con-temporary Christianity is to enable the re-connection of such convictions with a theological perspective upon human living, so that an appropriate self-belief can be re-discovered.

Protestantism's crucial contemporary protest must be against consumerism.

I have spoken of a style of 'protesting Christianity' as continuous with historical Protestantism which is not the preserve of Protestants alone. The days, though, have gone when it is the (Roman Catholic) Church or state princes against which protesting Christians must object. What, then, should be the main focus of contemporary, protesting Christianity? Out of the many possible contenders, I suggest that it is consumerism in relation to which thoughtful, critical Christianity must mainly define itself. By 'consumerism' here I mean what may be termed 'the triumph of economics' or 'the idolization of the material'. I do not deny that we all are, and must be, consumers, in that we use things, and – given the structure of western societies – buy things that we use. Consumerism understood as the triumph of economics or the idolization of the material means the extent to which we not only consume but are consumed by preoccupations with what we earn, spend or what we devote our leisure time to.

Two words of caution must be issued straightaway. First, this sounds like the comment of a wealthy person. In global terms, of course, I am indeed wealthy, even if by British standards I am not. But it is easy to summon people not to be preoccupied by economic, material concerns when one has a regular income. However, history shows that a wide range of people of different wealth backgrounds can reach the same insight: that preoccupation with wealth is destructive. Indeed, it could be argued that it is the poor who perceive it most clearly, as they do so without the material clutter which veils the eyes of the wealthy. In saying this, though, I have no desire to suggest that poverty is in itself holy. It may be. But even in my own limited experience I have seen too many cases of material poverty to believe that it is holy in any simple way.

A second cautionary word: opposition to consumerism should not be understood simply as the assertion of the importance of 'the spiritual' over against 'the material'. Through its commitment to belief in an incarnate God, Christianity is too materialist a religion to hide behind spirituality alone. What Christianity demands of itself and others is an appropriate understanding of the material world, one which values the material world as given by God. The inner and interrelated workings of the material world are not,

I let you go to,
Tesco —.

however, to be treated deterministically, as if human beings somehow had no contribution to make to the world's course. On the
contrary, if human beings are to be seen as co-workers with God in
the fashioning of the world's future, then this includes taking full
responsibility for economic management of the world, and for
appropriate environmentally aware use of the world's resources.[13]
The question then arises as to the principles according to which such
management is to occur.

It is time to develop a 'New Puritanism'.

At root, protesting Christianity should, in the present, invite people
to serious living. We may, if we wish, call it a 'New Puritanism'.
This would be mindful of, but not identical with, the old form. The
new form will not rely on the slogans of journalists all too ready to
label as 'puritan' anyone who questions their own licence, or is
cautious about the exercise and extent of their pleasure. It will have
done its homework properly. Puritans never were killjoys. They
simply thought deeply and seriously about how to live, believing
that the whole of their lives should be understood as being lived
before God. Ultimate meaning suffused every aspect of their life.
'New Puritanism' could thus encourage people new to Christianity
to consider living their lives in a similarly serious way, informed by
all the best traditions that Christianity has at its disposal.[14]

The late Erik Routley said much about this of Lichbook on the free churches.

Protestantism tends to produce wordy thinkers rather than pray-ers, but there is a rich vein of types of Protestant spirituality to be drawn on.

Do you prefer the flowing-bits?

Puritans, like most Protestants, were thoughtful preachers.
Preaching may have had its day as an art form in our present
culture.[15] But Protestantism will surely remain known especially as
a 'wordy' style of Christianity. Protestants have been known for
their hostility towards the visual, and their concern for the propositional over the imaginative. But even here the historical evidence is
mixed.[16] And it is currently the case that Protestant denominations
are rediscovering all kinds of ways of being more creative in their
worship than in the past (e.g., in the use of meditations, banners, art,
drama and dance). — *oh yes — I for one!*

!! Alas! And if we keep doing so it will but what will remain of the Protestant tradition?

But I hope not at the expense of the proclamation of the Word.

Even so, the wide range of Protestant spirituality should be attended to in any refreshing of Christianity in Britain today. If Protestantism has proved too wordy at times, nevertheless many of its words are worth reading. To draw on some simple and obvious examples just from the history of British Protestantism, one need only glance at many of the sections on 'Later Protestant Spirituality' in the excellent collection of essays, *The Study of Spirituality*, to be reminded of the resources which have come from British experience of Christianity itself.[17]

The emphasis on words in Protestantism relates to the stimulus of thought, as well as belief and practice.

The wordiness of Protestantism is a crucial feature of its keenness to press for clarity and profundity of thought. Despite the traditions and works of spirituality just referred to, Christianity in the Protestant tradition has at times been in danger of becoming over-intellectual. Not for nothing has western Protestantism produced so many scholars who have sought to order Christian belief in a systematic way (thus producing works of 'systematic theology'). Systematic thought is out of fashion. In some ways this is understandable. It smacks of control, neatness, absence of loose ends, unreality. It is not post-modern. It does not seem to mesh with real life as we now live it.

But systematic theology has a point. It presses for coherence (how does one bit of Christian belief fit with another?). And it demands of Christians the sharpest of critical reflection. At this juncture, a crucial aspect of liberalism's open, critical approach to Christianity merges with Protestantism's wordiness.

Clarity and coherence can also be regarded as hallmarks of a style of Christianity which affirms the value of critical rigour in religion. Protestantism will not be the only form of Christianity to press for this. But given its history it cannot avoid being one of the most prominent voices calling for such a critical approach.

Different types of Christianity will appeal to different psychological types.

A protesting style of Christianity, be it inside or outside of Protestantism, will not appeal to all. Different styles of Christianity clearly do appeal to different types of people. If I am choosing to offer an apologia for a new form of Liberal Protestantism in this book, I must accept that I may be saying simply: 'This has helped me, and my personality type, perhaps it will help you too.' I believe, however, that a new way of arguing a Liberal Protestant case is needed at the moment for a greater reason than that of appealing to a particular personality type. The forms of Christianity which do seem to be holding their own in Britain at present tend in two directions: the comfortable evangelical and the mysterious. The former is sustaining the relatively wealthy. The latter feeds the spirituality boom and offers a means of escape. There is little Christianity in Britain at present which moves much beyond an individualistic, quietist, apolitical spirituality. It does look as though Christianity has to look closely at the forms in which it is presenting itself, where its critical, protesting edge has gone, and what kinds of people feel drawn towards it.

Liberal Protestants need not be tentative about trying to persuade others to become Christians.

I finish this chapter on a perhaps surprising, missiological note. Liberal Protestantism does not have a good track record in attracting people to it.[18] Yet as a loose collection of traditions of critical, socially and politically engaged Christianity it offers avenues worth exploring. It is time that this style of Christianity became more mission-oriented, that is, willing to show why it is worth pursuing as a credible, contemporary style of Christian thinking, believing and acting. Liberal Christians are scarcely likely to become bold evangelists. But they could do more in articulating the positive aspects of their position, and in making clear within and beyond the Church why it may be useful for a critical, Liberal Protestant style of Christianity to be adopted by many more people in Britain today.

*   *   *

With this missiological twist in mind, in the final chapter I shall turn
to very concrete ways in which the (appropriately chastened) 'New
Liberal Protestantism' should be seen as a viable form of religion in
a post-atheist age.

[handwritten annotations, partially legible:]

I'm not too happy with this.
What has bothered to the tradition of
Gordon Rupp, Philip Watson, Rupert
Davies, Newton Flew:
Yet it is still important — those
of us who belong to that tradition
get nervous when the secretary of the
Methodist Faith and order Committee
makes no reference to it
whatever! Just then I'm
not, I think,
a 'liberal' Protestant,
but a Neo-
orthodox
liberal
Catholic!

Contemporary Christianity and the Possibility of Responsible Faith

If Christianity is to be refreshed in Britain, then it is necessary to show how and why anyone should bother with it. That has been the basic question behind the whole of this book. Whether people are to look at Christianity for the first time, or return to it after a long period of non-attachment, a case has to be made for the value of a person taking such a step. In this final chapter, I present a series of discussion starters which turns the case for a New (Chastened) Liberal Protestantism into a set of concrete issues and concerns. These enable Christianity to be discerned as a viable option for contemporary living.

In an age when we're in danger of 'amusing ourselves to death', we must ensure that we keep in touch with things that matter most.

The phrase 'amusing ourselves to death' comes from the American communication studies professor and cultural commentator Neil Postman. His trenchant 1985 study bears that title, and deals with the damaging effect of television upon public discourse and cultural life.[1] One need not be anti-television or élitist with regard to popular culture to feel the force of his arguments. Postman demonstrates how the medium of television and the culture of the sound-bite have led to oversimplification of complex issues. Post-modern respect for surface rather than depth is, in Postman's world of media studies, seen to be reflected in a disregard for issues of truth. Religion itself is rightly not immune from Postman's critique. Simply attending to spiritual matters does not of itself mean that worship of the superficial is avoided.

Of course, it may be argued that there is no depth to life, and that all is indeed surface. Perhaps we do indeed wholly construct our own selves. Perhaps we really 'are' only the sum of our interactions with others. Perhaps the medium is not only the message, but the whole truth. Perhaps all of these conclusions, which are part of so much of the post-modern mood of contemporary culture, really are 'true'. What 'really matters' then is that we set about the creative construction of our own selves in an age of sheer amusement. But it is at this point that the tide begins to turn. Such a mood is the apotheosis of individualism. To question it is therefore to begin to ask the question 'What really matters?' rather differently. Granted, 'what really matters' will depend on who you ask, and in what context. But the first part of a constructive argument for the value of any religion in British society begins precisely here: it is worth asking long-established religions what matters most, as they have something major to contribute. Religions can help people find a way out of the concern that we really are in danger of missing the point of life, in a quagmire of rather unfulfilling entertainment. In the same way that people say, when on holiday, 'I could spend my whole life like this' without really meaning it, so also people can be challenged by religion to think of what matters most. Death, meaningful relationships, balanced living, care of one's body and the earth, thoughtful action, concern for other people (not just one's own kind), all of these aspects of human life can be stimulated by religious practice and belief. Similarly, religion can at its best enable people to discover means by which and resources through which many negative experiences of life (ill health, work crises, redundancy, failures in personal relationships) can be faced, and even worked beyond. Recognizing that religion can help here is thus a good place to start.

Religion is therapy for those of us who can't, or don't want to, afford expensive therapists.

There is a clear sense in which religion is therapeutic. All of the concerns which take people into counselling are touched on within a life of faith. The framework of belief within which one lives, moves and has one's being provides the working narrative in relation to which one lives one's own life (constructing your own life story as you go). 'God', as communicated by and embodied within whichever religious group one belongs to, is the therapist. But 'God' has to remain in inverted commas precisely because the concept of God with which any group works is always open to scrutiny. It is hoped (and believed) that God, in all of God's fundamental and awesome reality, is truly the therapist. But religion is at all times human *and* divine and pays the price for God's being incarnate. Human grasp of God's very presence is therefore subject to the vagaries of the created world.

Religion can, though, also create some of the neuroses that most of us live with. Precisely because religion touches on the nervous system of life (our sense of self and self-worth, emotions, memories, values), this makes the picture of what religion can and cannot do more complex. For how can religion be both salvific and damaging at one and the same time? But it is. And so long as religious people go through life in the company of good friends (whether religious or not), they can usually get by.

Religion is therefore therapy, even if a therapeutic model is of itself not enough to explain what religion achieves. 'Religion as therapy' relates well to an understanding of religion focused upon the securing of personal (i.e., individual) salvation. It is less useful a model to adopt in thinking of the political function of religion.

But Christianity undoubtedly needs to work harder at rebuffing the charges that all religions do is screw you up, and build on the discoveries which some psychologists have made on the basis of empirical study: religious belief can actually enable people to lead more balanced and mentally healthy lives than those who profess no religion. It is time to start saying this a bit louder.

It is a mistake to build a viable form of contemporary religion on supernaturalism.

Religion will not, though, contribute to people's enjoyment of a healthy and balanced life if they are expected to believe a hundred impossible things before breakfast. Too often religions have implied this, and Christianity is no exception. If this sounds like the voice of a liberal modernist giving in to the wisdom of secular rationality, then so be it. I make no apology and simply refer my critics to the next point below.

By 'supernaturalism' I mean the same as Steve Bruce, when he logs the decline of interest in the supernatural as one of the two key features of secularization brought about in large part by the Reformation.[2] There is no doubt that beliefs about who God was/is and what God can do have changed radically throughout the past few centuries. This can indeed be termed the extension of the monotheistic 'simplification of the supernatural' which was built into Judaism and Christianity from the start. Unlike Bruce, however, I do not see that the major shift from the supernatural to the natural in the modern and post-modern periods either makes God redundant or religion defunct.[3] It would, however, be right to follow Bruce in accepting that the re-focusing of religion in the contemporary world must resist playing supernatural games. Of course it must remain true that any kind of belief in God is 'supernatural' in the sense that a belief is held in that which is not seen, and not open to empirical testing. But the modern period reveals the extent to which religion must work in closer harmony with the findings of human disciplines such as the natural sciences, psychology and sociology, in accordance with the view that God works in and through natural processes and not outside of them.

At their best, religions respect and preserve a sense of mystery and awe in human living. They do not necessarily require the maintenance of belief that natural processes are bypassed. The role of religions is to enable people to live life whilst respecting and preserving that mystery and awe, without requiring the sacrificing of the intellect, and making full use of whatever knowledge is available. Post-modern caution about how much knowledge is available will, however, temper modernist assumptions about neutrality, definitiveness and objectivity in human knowledge.

It is equally a mistake to build a viable form of religion on the assumption that religion is a wholly human creation.

To question an inappropriate form of supernaturalism in religion (e.g., the notion that God could stop volcanoes erupting) is not the same as denying the existence of God, or as claiming that religion is simply a human creation. We do, of course, shape the religions we hold. We make things up as we try to grasp what reality is like, and how we should live. Sometimes we are not sure which of the narratives used in religions are fiction and which are fact. Sometimes the categories 'fiction' and 'fact' are inadequate to characterize religions' stories.[4] However, even accepting that we do make things up, it is quite mistaken to suppose that religions are not seeking to relate to, and in some sense describe, reality 'as it is'. The only point at issue is the forms in which reality is being understood. Religions handle reality indirectly, obliquely, as befits the mysterious life we have to live.

Churches do not have, and never have had, a monopoly on truth, even though the 'Christendom model' of Christianity has been able to operate as if this were the case. Lots of different bodies and movements will help us work out what to think and believe, and how to behave.

To argue that religion can help people try and work out what matters most and to lead healthy lives does not mean that any one religion can and should try to do this alone. The case for commending Christianity therefore accepts pluralism as not merely inevitable but also profoundly useful. Admittedly, the prospect of trying to be religious (and in all likelihood, for sanity's sake, working out of one main religious tradition) in the midst of many competing, and sometimes conflicting, world-views is quite frightening. But that is how things are. Though a challenge, pluralism prevents Christians living in ghettoes. The range of life issues to which religion can relate (as spelt out in Chapter 1) will be handled in some way by whatever religious tradition one primarily stands within. As a context, pluralism will prevent any single version of Christianity controlling a person's whole worldview, and question Christianity's claim to any lazy absoluteness. Such a situation is as it should be if God is held to be God of the whole created order.

In a fragmented, yet tradition-saturated, age, it is vital to make choices about particular world-views, communities and groups which it is worth attaching oneself to.

A plural, post-modern, fragmented world – and a sackful of conflicting world-views – presents a huge challenge. But in the same way that a limitless pluralism is unwelcome (because it is ultimately untenable), so also the absence of any firm commitments on the part of contemporary British citizens is undesirable. I noted in Chapter 2 how all human beings live within traditions (whether aware of it or not). The co-existence of multiple and sometimes unclear world-views merely suggests the importance of doing some disentangling, and of some commitment making. Rather than accept what's given to us, it should surely be imperative that we ask awkward questions of the world-views we inhabit. In the interests not only of individual well-being, but of social stability, collective flourishing, and moral goodness, it is crucial that we know which world-views we inhabit and why. The question of whether a religious commitment would be beneficial – personally, socially and politically – must arise. If it does not, then we have a right to ask whether or not our culture is being spiritually abused through the neglect of religion. The specific question as to whether a commitment to Christianity would be advisable, is merely a specific form of this question.

'Attachment' to a world-view, community or group means being able to specify a particular form of loyal commitment, otherwise it means little.

I have switched from talk of 'commitment' to talk of 'attachment' here. As studies of British and American society both show, people are less likely than in the past to commit themselves to causes or groups. This lack of commitment finds expression in an unwillingness to become members of organizations. As one reviewer of a recent study of this aspect of American culture summarizes:

> Americans no longer frequent bowling alleys to bowl together in local leagues. More and more the aisles are full of individuals playing on their own.[5]

We might even add 'if they are full at all'. Recalling the first point made in this chapter, it may be more likely that people stay at home watching television.

Commitments will not, though, have much real effect in life unless people do something about them. This means turning a commitment into an attachment, a membership, an act of concrete belonging. It is not surprising that 'Christian commitment' has needed to be measured by 'church-going'. Yet church-going creates a contemporary dilemma in western culture. Its decline has understandably been interpreted as a loss of commitment. And yet as a social habit, it is not, in many of its present forms, welcome to all who are/would be Christians. It is problematic, further, given the evolution of the 'weekend' in western culture.

But if commitment is to be recovered, then some kind of attachment will be needed lest individualism in religion be perpetuated. If it is not 'church-going' in its current form which can supply this need, the question is: What can supply the need? The question invites the Christianity of the future to look in at least two directions. First, we need to look (as many Christians in western culture have admittedly tried to do over the past four or five decades) at what alternative, viable patterns of Christian community there may be to traditionally understood forms of church-going. Second, we need to ask about the nature and value of Christianity's interaction with (and interpretation of) the primary forms of community we do enjoy, for example, families, friendships, interest and political groups, work teams.

Commitment to Christianity will entail making specific commitment to particular forms and understandings of Christianity.

As well as pressing for specificity in Christian commitment in terms of concrete attachment to a body of people, however, it is important to highlight how the commitment will take shape as Christian commitment. If traditional church-going is to be qualified as the primary, or only, form in which a Christian attachment is established and measured, it is nevertheless crucial that worship, prayer and theological reflection occur in some way.

Denominations will, of course, continue. They may change radically within themselves, and via the new alliances which will form. In Britain it is, for example, surely inconceivable that in the future the Church of England and the Methodist Church will remain as detached from each other as they have done for so long. Trilateral talks keep the Church of England, the Methodist Church and the United Reformed Church in touch with each other. Though these are formal, national level discussions, such conversations have local implications, even if it takes time for these repercussions to occur.

The LEP's are very important.

Traditional church-going will continue for some, probably for many. Any new initiatives will surely be parasitic on such structures, and it will be important that this is so. It will also be frustrating, as new initiatives challenge both orthodoxies and established habits, and both challenges are painful. But as there is no such thing as tradition-less Christianity (because there is no such thing as tradition-less human life), the parasitic nature of any new forms of Christian community will simply have to be accepted. The greater question is whether the denominations themselves can cope with it.

More broadly, people will need to immerse themselves in the riches of Christianity's resources, whether within specific denominational channels or not, in order to find help in saying what they need to say: about God, the world, themselves, Christ, human beings, creation, the spirit, etc. We may live in post-denominational times (yet see Bruce on this!), but we do not live in post-traditional times. The particularity and necessity of tradition/s cannot be side-stepped if resources are to be found and used in a constructive manner. Consistency and coherence is helped when people dip into the same well time and again. You go back to where you regularly find water, whatever kind of well it be (denominational, Protestant, liberation, liberal, evangelical or whatever).

There will have to be new forms of 'church'.

As many people are now recognizing, though, new forms of 'church' will be needed. If commitment means attachment, and attachment entails belonging, then social forms need to be found for Christians and would-be Christians to connect with others in the Christian praise of, and search for, God. But if traditional patterns of church-going are not working, or cannot be made to work, for all, then the finding of new forms is a contemporary imperative. Much is made of 'cell churches', Christian communities who exist primarily in small group form, in relation to which the gathered church is then the larger (but secondary) body.[6] These are important, and the model is surely vital. It is, however, not clear that the cell church movement has the theological flexibility to sustain the many styles of Christianity which exist. It is a little suspicious that cell churches usually seem to be evangelical, and have a certain kind of 'strong' (and often male) leadership.

As a model, cell churches imitate a past strength of my own tradition – the Methodist. Whether Methodism can or should ever again find something akin to the 'class system' (i.e., a system of 'classes' or 'groups') through which its members related deeply with a small group of believers, and within which, at the groups' best, they found friendship and opportunity for faith-exploration, is a moot point.[7] But it does nevertheless seem quite clear that a new diversity of patterns of belonging will be needed for Christianity to offer a viable structure in relation to which people can organize their lives.

It is a comparatively recent problem for Christians to have to think about how to shape their religious life. Sunday had always been Sunday. And until the 1960s it had only been the wealthy who had many social alternatives to what churches provided in some localities. Churches provided everything for those who belonged to them in the immediate post-war period. By contrast, 'church' now has to be made to fit into the rather different social patterns (of work, family life, friendships, leisure, holidays) that people have. The challenge, therefore, is to discover how to deal with contemporary life in a way in which Christian faith can still play a role, whilst recognizing that participation in a Christian community will occur very differently from in the past.

Worship will take new forms, and will often not take place on Sundays.

One obvious consequence of the call to a different form of church is the impact this will inevitably have on Sunday worship. Patterns are already changing. But in the future it will surely not be the case that mainstream denominations will assume a Sunday morning service to function automatically as the focal point of their communal life. The '10.30 Eucharist' or the '11 o'clock morning service' may well remain fixtures for many years. But churches offering such services may have to accept that they will be attended by their older members, whilst Wednesday at 8 p.m., Friday at 9 p.m. and Sunday at 4 p.m. become similar fixed points for different groups. What is more, a pattern of personal spirituality seeking to balance individual prayer and reflection with corporate worship may be developed which accepts that an individual may 'connect' with a group only on a monthly basis. This is not necessarily about Christianity demanding

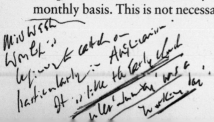

less of its members than in the past. It is a matter of contemporary Christianity adjusting how it makes its appropriate demands on people whose lifestyles are very different.

A Christian may, for instance, be part of a small group which meets weekly locally where she lives or at her place of work, participate on a monthly basis in a larger eucharistic service, and also have a daily pattern of personal prayer. Another may have a pattern of worship once a month, attend a regional (cathedral) service each quarter and undertake a retreat once a year. There are many possible such structures. Only on a very negative and pessimistic reading of this development could it be regarded as damagingly individualistic. It is better to see it as a necessary part of religious change.

Furthermore, the type of worship conducted will surely continue to develop in its variety. There have been bold attempts at so-called 'alternative worship' throughout the 1980s and 1990s, some of which failed badly.[8] But such efforts merely responded to the failure of much traditional worship to connect with a younger age-group. That 'younger age-group' now amounts to the under-fifties in British culture. Some of those under-fifties, as I noted earlier (in Chapter 3), have turned to quite traditional, liturgical (including medieval) forms of Christian worship in their need to find a tradition. This has even been a feature of some of the alternative worship, in which Latin has come back into fashion. But silence, art, film, a vast range of music, computer-generated images, small groups, participative forms, chanting, conversational Bible studies, readings and discussions are all going to feature in future styles of Christian worship. One of the biggest challenges, of course, in the age of the game show, will be when and how to use technology appropriately, and what the role of the 'compere' should be.

'Commitment to Christianity' may mean many things.

It is going to be more necessary in the future to accept that people stumble into Christianity, and even stay there, for all sorts of different reasons. I know plenty of people who are in churches now mainly because the church has provided their entire life structure since the 1950s. If they had lived as teenagers in the 1980s, rather than the 1950s, then things would surely have been different. The social alternatives which the 1980s supplied were simply not available in 1950s Britain.

It may still prove true, though, that people will find themselves within Christianity even now for reasons which do not at first seem wholly to do with religion, for example, because their baby was named in church (in what just happens to have been a service of baptism), because it provides a kind of social life, because it is one of the few socially and politically committed bodies in the neighbourhood, or because it is a communal focal point. They have not come within the reach of Christianity, in other words, for any major ethical, theological or ideological reason. But this simply highlights the need for such an encounter with Christianity to begin to function ethically and theologically for them, even whilst fulfilling the functions for which they find a Christian group helpful.

Two observations are important here. First, the contrast between the 1950s and the 1980s masks an important similarity. Because there are nevertheless still people who have stumbled into Christianity for various reasons, we need to remember that the Church has been full of half-believers, agnostics, the confused, and the theologically unconfident for some time. This will not be a new thing. People in the Church and outside it need reminding that churches are not, in actual fact, full of ranks of the certain or the bold. Second, even allowing for this potential similarity, there is no doubting the relative absence of so many people from churches. The argument for involvement in Christianity thus has to begin, as this book began, with the question of what would persuade anyone to include 'Christian community' alongside the many groups they might be attached to. Unlike the approach of much Christian evangelism, which tends to want to get people to believe, it might be more advisable to start elsewhere. Why should people devote time to this? Why should people belong to such a group? Asking such questions in a context where it can be accepted that people affiliate themselves to churches for all sorts of reasons may be more positive.

'Commitment to God' can mean many things.

More fundamentally, there is no escaping the fact that people seem to mean very different things by 'God'. Even when espousing the most straightforward orthodoxy, and being more than happy to recite authorized creeds, believers diverge the moment they try and put into their own words precisely what they mean by the various clauses of the creeds. And certainly, as an adult education exercise I have used with Christians over many years has proved, believers differ radically as to which clauses of the creeds are the more important.

For some, 'God' remains the angry judge. God's primary concern is to dictate about moral right and wrong. For others, 'God' is the benevolent parent, who will rarely (if ever) scold. The loving arms are warm and welcoming. For yet others, 'God' is (abstract) love, and Love then becomes God. Overlapping with these three are a number of other ideas and images. God is the one who suffers, the one who gives life, is Power, is Spirit, fosters relationships, is a close friend, is a distant Force. Christians say all these things, sometimes revealing the extent to which their God-concept is informed by their understanding of Jesus Christ, sometimes not.

My current paid work brings me alongside those who have responsibility (as the Faith and Order Committee) for overseeing the doctrine and worship of the Methodist Church in Great Britain. At one level the collective task we have is very simple. As an orthodox denomination within post-Reformation Protestantism, adhering to the classical creeds, with a clearly defined founding statement (the Deed of Union of 1932) and a whole host of authoritative statements to work with, we must simply work out whether any new developments are consistent or inconsistent with the tradition within which we all stand. At the same time, we are all clearly aware of the practical difficulties of our task. Orthodoxy is not the same as what people actually believe. What people believe may not always be healthy (but who decides, and what do you do about it?). But orthodoxy may not always be healthy either. The latter is harder to shift, of course. But seismic shifts have happened in Christian thought and practice, even whilst the creeds have (by and large) remained the same for centuries.

Because human living requires traditions, then orthodoxy is necessary. Because orthodoxy does not simply describe what people actually believe, but tries both to shape and to respond to challenges from those beliefs, then we can only speak of a 'generous ortho-doxy'.[9] It is, though, crucial to recognize just how different people's notions of God can be.

The 'agnostic onlookers' and 'theological non-realists' must not be excluded from the Christian search for God.

Agnostics are those who don't know whether or not there is a God. Theological non-realists are those who deem it crucially important that 'God-language' be used in human speech, but don't believe that God 'is' outside of human speech or experience. The latter could be called 'atheists' (who don't believe that God exists, or that God-language is important) but that wouldn't be fair to them. What they disbelieve is the notion of some God 'out there' (whether a bearded man in the sky, or a spiritual reality within). My hunch is that there are more non-realists in Christianity than are willing to own up, but that some of those relatively few who call themselves non-realists may be more 'realist' (i.e., God 'is') than they care to admit.

Be that as it may, my earlier statement that 'the Church has been full of half-believers, agnostics, the confused, and the theologically unconfident for some time' must be extended and tweaked a bit further. Agnostic onlookers and theological non-realists must not be excluded from the Christian search for God. Indeed, it should be accepted that they are likely already to be an integral part of organized Christianity. They should be welcomed in Christian communities. We are, in all probability, always shifting positions anyway, even those of us who profess a firm(-ish) faith. So to include amongst the community (or communities) of faith those who are still trying to find faith should not be a surprise.

My guess that there are many *de facto* agnostics and non-realists sitting in churches week in and week out is not merely an expression of hope. It is more a reflection on the evident questioning and searching that people do in private, or in contexts other than in the life of the church. For example, when undertaking formal qualifications in theology and religious studies, or in more informal settings, people are willing to open up much more to the impact upon faith exploration of their actual fears, questions, doubts, insights, experiences. There are, of course, plenty more 'agnostic onlookers' and 'theological non-realists' outside organized Christianity. The large overlap between those who are faith strugglers in the church, and those who might be sympathetic to faith, but lie beyond churches, has long been known to be considerable. It may now be less than it was. But this should be a cause for concern less because of the size of the identifiable Church, and more because of what the absence of

Clement was once asked
Gitber whether he was an agnostic
whether he was an agnostic
'I don't know' he said!

faith exploration would mean for the well-being of society and its individual members. Religion matters not simply as a social force. It matters because it is a major contributor to society members' exploration of life's meaning/s, their own selves, their goals and their own, society's and the world's ultimate end.

Faith exploration has to be a possibility for those who are not sure what to make of 'God'. Churches may not, in the present, manage to do this as churches (at least in their present form), or do it very well. But they need to maximize opportunities to encourage faith exploration wherever it may be done, for the sake of individual and communal well-being. Faith and theology matter for society.

We must accept that religions are in the business of trying to identify and articulate something more than is given an account of by sociologists of religion.

Religions can contribute to communal well-being and thus to the re-making of civil society. Religious people are bound to think that religions will be crucial for this. Our job is to show how and why this is so. Christians will want to show that Christianity has a particular contribution to make. It need not be an exclusive contribution. But it may prove distinctive. Neither the variety of religious contributions, nor any particular Christian contribution, can, however, be accounted for simply on the basis of what religions achieve socially and politically. Though some people may be religious and may be church-goers for reasons which are not always identifiably religious, the fact that religions deal with much more than the factors which keep the believers together means that the sociologists can't be allowed to have the last word about what religions achieve. Religions connect with all of the features of human living which were touched on in Chapter 1. They supply much 'social capital', that is, the cultural preconditions by which societies prosper. But they handle psychological and metaphysical 'capital' too, both of which are needed for human flourishing.

**Christians will need a portable faith capable of being expressed
and enriched much more flexibly than most current models of
Christian thought and practice will find comfortable.**

We may, then, speak of a 'portable faith'. Christians need a belief in
God which they carry with them as they live their lives. This faith
affects all dimensions of their life. It shapes and interprets their
communal living and the decisions they make about moral action.
But it does not contain any simple blueprint for a form of 'church'
to provide the communal support for that faith, even though a
communal aspect will be needed. Christianity has, in other words,
moved beyond assuming that 'faith' and 'church' (or at least, the
Church as we know it) easily belong together, even whilst recognizing that faith needs communal expression.

Conversely, the 'portable faith' which Christians need must be a
personal faith without being individualistic. It must neither turn
believers in on themselves (the old problem of Protestant self-
absorption) or ignore the fact that faith needs nourishment from
other Christians in the present, and from forms of past Christianity.
The portability does not, in other words, mean that believers control
the content of belief. Otherwise we're back with the lingering suspi-
cion about liberal Christianity – that it enables believers to believe
what they like. 'Portable faith' can call in at many filling stations.
This is unlikely to happen wholly randomly. But one concession to
the socially mobile, fragmented age which Christianity will have to
make is to recognize that denominational loyalty cards are seen as
less valuable than they once were. People aren't terribly worried
about collecting spiritual points from one petrol company, even
whilst they know that regular fill-ups are needed.

**The traditions and groups to which Christians are attached and
committed will need to challenge, as well as support and enrich,
Christians, otherwise individual Christians could simply control
the content of their faith, and their understanding of God.**

The groups to which Christians of the future relate will need to be
groups which challenge as well as support believers. Christians
whose primary group is located, say, at their place of work will
receive help and support as they interpret their working life in the

How?

light of their faith in God. But it will be inadequate as a primary Christian group if it fails to help those who meet within it to interpret the rest of their lives, and to look at understandings of faith quite different from the ones that their place of work requires of them. Fragmented, portable Christianity, in other words, accentuates the contextual nature of all Christian belief more than has usually been required in the history of the Church. Positively expressed, fragmented, portable Christianity demands that Christians learn from other Christians, through making them directly aware of the limited reach of their own faith and context.

We are getting too Vaguer.

Within an understanding of church as a 'network of networks' Christianity can in future be a network of groups, formal and informal, of varying styles of Christianity.

The consequence of these developments is that it is better to see Christianity much more as a complex network of networks, than as large-scale institutions (churches). Denominations and institutional churches will continue to exist. But Christianity will function more and more through a mixture of such formally organized groups and many more informal, loosely affiliated groups which attach themselves to such structures. These are not 'para-church groups' in the sense that they consciously try to run parallel to churches and then end up imitating or competing with them. They will exist within and across identifiable churches, for example, as cell groups, as fellowship groups, as study groups, as work-related groups, or as groups set up in hospitals, YMCAs, chaplaincies, businesses. They are likely to become more and more significant as time goes on, as the main focal points at which people's Christian faith surfaces, is expressed and explored.

In my own tradition, Methodism, the notion of 'connexionalism' – the interlocking and mutually supporting nature of all churches – has always been present in Britain. It has arguably remained better as theory than as a practice. Or it has worked when seen as a tendency to centralize, and to control from the centre. But at its best, it is a view of church already as a network, which encourages all believers to see their own group as limited in scope, and needing other groups in order to be church. This seems an appropriate model for a viable future structure of Christianity in Britain.

This assumes a Wesleyan mould. De ulh's 5 pm's were much less connexional!

I do with we would stop using this silly phrase.

The consequence of such a development for the structure of 'ministry' is, of course, colossal. But it is surely right and proper that forms of ministry evolve which fit existing patterns of Christian community than vice versa. The point I make here is neither that Christianity can be unstructured, nor that clergy are superfluous. I am simply extending the implications of what is already beginning to happen to Christianity in Britain, and needs to happen more if Christianity is to connect with the developments which are happening in spirituality.

Marg note: WHO PAYS?
Marg note: Paish Never mention Money!

The involvement in 'the Christian community' of an individual Christian (in whatever form and at whatever point the individual exercises that contact) must lead to creative theological interpretation of that individual's participation in other relationships and communities.

Marg note: why use a Word like that!

A future form for Christian faith must not, though, now become ecclesiocentric (church-centred) via the back door. It must not be thought that noting the importance of an inevitably communal dimension to Christian faith, of the identification of a primary group, and then of the interweaving of such groups with forms of the Church as we know it, means that everything revolves around 'church' after all. At this point, the new face of Christianity – as the combination of a portable, personal faith and a socially committed world-view – becomes clear. Christian faith does not merely give people a body to relate to (a Christian community). It asks that people assess all of the social contexts in which they live their lives in the light of Christian faith. And it urges them to think how any of the social contexts in which they live their lives might help them understand Christian faith, and thus the workings of God amongst people in the world.

Here I can cite an example that at present confronts me every week. Our son plays for a junior football team. Founded over thirty years ago as a social club alongside a Roman Catholic church, it is now a large-scale independent organization, running nine teams. It is a rival to churches in so far as its games are mostly played on Sundays. To begin with, this meant our son's unavailability for much of the year for church activities. My wife and I decided it would be right to let him play, for the sake of friendships, physical health and also so that 'church' did not come to dominate his life without him having much say about it.

It quickly became apparent that the club was a rival to the church in a different sense. It is not too far from the truth to say that of the people who ventured out of the house at all on Sunday mornings in our part of town, whilst the over-fifties were in churches, the under-fifties were watching or playing football. The atmosphere pitch-side is convivial, sometimes passionate. The sense of belonging and well-being is palpable, sometimes more so than in the life of churches. Equally, the same, basic issues of human dynamics are present as in churches: Who's fallen out with whom? Who's got power? Who wants power? Who's actually doing the work? Who's not pulling their weight? *Surprise! Surprise!*

Now this example may qualify a basic assumption which has run throughout this book – that people don't get committed to things any more. For don't we have here an example of something to which people will commit themselves, when the well-being and advancement of their children is concerned? And isn't this commitment echoed in other areas of life, especially sport, when people show commitment to a cause (e.g., their team)? I have, however, acknowledged from the start that people do devote time to many things, whilst suggesting at the same time that patterns of commitment have undoubtedly shifted.

Even so, my point is not simply to say – as might have been done by forms of so-called 'secular theology' thirty or forty years ago – that the football club is merely 'church' by another name. This would be a wrong line to take. The football club is not a church, even whilst it fulfils some of the functions of church. It has no explicit theology, even whilst some of its functions enable its members (and those who benefit from it) to receive something of the grace of God through the quality of the relationships, and the sense of well-being, which the club fosters. My purpose is to note the value of a mutually critical dialogue between an identifiable form of corporate Christian life, and a different form of communal human life. Whatever form of Christian community people might participate in, it will need to function in some way as a context out of which the rest of life can be interpreted.

One feature in favour of the football club over (sadly) too many churches is that people seem to do their best to be friendly towards one another. This is made more possible simply because more time

ask Roy Keane!

is spent in one another's company, and there is more time than churches often allow to get to know who you're standing next to, how their week has gone, or how their job or search for work is progressing. By contrast, the football club is unlike a church in restricting its membership quite savagely: to a limited-sized squad of physically able players. In this respect, Christian groups – if they function in practice as they should, and are open to all – behave quite differently.

This is a simple example, and is one which could be extended in many directions: towards family, work teams, hobby groups, political parties, music clubs, groups of friends. Without the mutual interplay between forms of Christian community and the communal contexts of daily life, then Christian faith remains individualistic (as the private possession of an individual believer) or ghettoized (locked away in a church separated from settings in which the bulk of life is lived). When Christian community and other communal contexts of daily life are allowed to dialogue with each other, then the whole of life can be enriched.

Does that Church have Youth work at some other time? or what? [handwritten]

Religions will need to take their educative role more seriously, not simply in terms of 'grooming people in the faith', but in making their own contribution to people's understanding of how important religion is in British society.

There is, though, one further step which Christianity will have to make if it is to make headway in Britain in the future. Not only must Christianity enable Christians to use their faith to interpret the rest of their lives. It must also contribute to their education about religion's role in British society. It could even be said (as is said of knowledge of languages) that a person who knows only one faith knows none.[10] Christians will therefore need to play a role in fashioning the Christian religion as a 'lifelong learning community' not simply to groom people in Christian faith, but also to respect and explore the Christian religion as one religion amongst many in Britain.

This educational necessity can go in many directions. Christians will certainly need to be encouraged to take full advantage of available educational awards (GCSEs, A-Levels, University degrees, Open Theological College and Open Learning Centre Courses) to

How? When? If the Church is so vague, how can all this be done. [handwritten]

be informed about religions and about Christianity. Churches can also more and more become venues where education and training take place (not only in and about religion). Christian groups and individuals can themselves join in partnerships with educational bodies to ensure that Christians and others are offered high quality training and education. As I noted earlier in this book, there have long been calls for better and more widespread 'laity training'. Perhaps we can now see that this has to be included within an even bigger vision: of Christian education within the Church, but also education in and beyond the Church in Christianity and other religious traditions. Only via such a route can the inevitable place of religions within a healthy future society be adequately explored.

Fine – but who does it?

Local forms of religion (e.g., Christian churches) need to be contexts in which people have doors opened up to the wider world.

Education, education, education: it remains the plaintive cry of the liberal. We know it will not solve everything. And not everyone wants to be educated, or links with the Christian religion in order to be educated. Participation in a religious tradition remains educative nevertheless. One crucial area in which this occurs is through a religion's capacity to enable a believer to perceive the global in the local, and the whole in the part. Participation in a religion will always be a concrete affair, as I have stressed throughout this book. It can never be anything but local: involving participation in a real, concrete, embodied group of believers. But because religion always addresses the ultimate, it not only looks beyond the local, it takes in the global too. If local participation does not require this of a believer, then religious belief and practice is being left incomplete. Religions are not 'world religions' for nothing, and metaphysics is not universal in scope to no end.

Christianity, then, needs to be a channel through which Christians, in being opened up to God, are also confronted with, and choose to wrestle with, contemporary global issues.

Through their involvement in religion locally, people will be encouraged to reflect on, as well as participate in, the things that matter locally.

In turn, the global affects the local. Enriched by the encounter with global issues, and informed by the thinking of Christians beyond their immediate locality (elsewhere in Britain, and from around the world), Christians will be enabled to look at their own local setting quite differently. In this way, Christian faith's impact upon local politics and community issues can be seen to occur not just through what people have experienced locally. Christianity is one of the channels through which a broader and more critically analytical view can be taken of issues which matter locally.

Christianity will only reveal itself to be a viable form of religion in contemporary Britain if it begins to work again for people as a source of personal, social and political transformation.

And so to the last thesis, one which functions as a summary of the whole book, and yet sounds like a tall order. It is clear that a new form of Christianity has to be found. It will be like and unlike the old. It must draw on the past. It will worship the same God. But it will move beyond the contemporary churches in ways in which it is currently difficult to foresee. And it will carry people with it in ways we cannot yet quite envisage. To call them 'passengers' is too insulting. For everyone is riding together anyway. There are very few drivers.

   Christianity's future viability, however, will need to mesh with continued evidence that personal encounter with Christian traditions, in the company of other Christians and those seeking some kind of faith, can continue to be life-enhancing. This can undoubtedly happen. But as this book has suggested, it is not just a matter of Christianity presenting itself better (though it includes that too). It is also a matter of clearing the way so that the question of religion is again seen to be a serious one, and one that contemporary British society cannot afford not to pose.

Responsible Christian faith thus reveals itself to be not the mere learning of a set of texts or practices, not simply an attitude driven by conviction politics, and not just belonging to a church. Responsible Christian faith entails 'inhabiting' a tradition, participation in a group, within a community, whilst wrestling alongside others with a way of viewing the world as lived wholly before God. Whoever and whatever God proves to be, whilst people live within the Christian theological tradition, they maintain hope, value others and recognize their interdependence with them, interpret the whole of their lives through a particular lens of meaning and exercise appropriate reserve about what human beings can and cannot achieve. As a way of living, this theological approach to life shapes individual practice and contributes to the social well-being both of the believer and of wider society. If this potential of Christianity can find a new way of being discovered in contemporary Britain, then the continuing public importance of religion will merely be confirmed in practice. This road – a spacious and inviting thoroughfare, even if not a broad highway – rather than that leading to the continued privatization of religion, or the one which simply accepts Christianity's continued decline, is the one to follow.

Epilogue

'New Christianity'

This book almost received the title 'New Christianity'. It would have been a rhetorical device – a gimmick, even – to attract the potential reader and purchaser. There can, though, be no 'new Christianity' in the sense that Christianity can be wholly re-invented. 'New Christianity' sounds, in any case, too good to be true. There have been forms of 'New Theology' and 'New Evangelism' before. There was a publication called *New Christian* in the 1960s. They came and went. In the present in Britain we wrestle with the meanings of 'New Labour', 'New Britain' and 'New Man'. 'New Christianity', then, sounds too faddish for its own good.

But let me be frank. This book has an unashamedly missionary purpose. It has arisen from my sense that too many people are getting through their lives in Britain today without giving religion, and Christianity, a serious look. In fact, the situation is worse than this. People are reacting to Christianity in response to very meagre and partial versions of it. Or they are barely encountering it at all. Put this alongside the impact of some of the aspects of secularization I highlighted in Chapter 2, and you could even say that many in Britain today are suffering spiritual abuse. This is not, as many of the vigorous critics of Christianity and religion would have it, because Christians and others go round badgering people. Quite the opposite is the case. People are suffering the abuse of spiritual neglect: the notion that all is done when the minimum of thinking is undertaken about how to live (a bit of ethics), but the maximum is undertaken to acquire wealth (a lot of economics).

I parody only slightly. The quest for meaningful, paid work is, of course, more than a matter of getting cash. It is about dignity and well-being, often not just for oneself, but also for dependents. However, what's often missing – in work, family life, education, leisure, local politics – is critical reflection on the values by which people are currently operating. Where reflection is happening (e.g., health care, social, youth and community work) is precisely the place where 'spirituality' is being rediscovered, and where the input of religious professionals, acting as the right kind of 'theological informants', is proving profoundly valuable.

But as is often said, religion is much too important to be left to the professionals. If there is a single main thread running through this book, it is this: that the riches of Christianity need rediscovering by a great many more people, in new forms, and for a variety of ends (personal, social, political, national) in Britain today. This is not just for the sake of the continuation of Christianity, or its churches. It is certainly not just for the sake of individual Christians. It is not even simply to get the country running more smoothly, socially and politically. All three would result from a widespread, committed engagement with Christianity by many people. But let's face it: not everyone is going to become Christian. Muslims, Hindus, Buddhists, Jews, Sikhs, Jains, Baha'is should certainly not be expected to. Those of no religious persuasion may not choose to either. But some may never have given religion a thought. A re-think is in order. The threat of eternal damnation does not work any more, and should not be tried (whatever the truth may be, it is not a good advertisement for God). But an argument based on a combination of the personal, social, political and metaphysical well-being of oneself and others will have more going for it.

Being concerned for a 'New Christianity', a revitalized Christianity, then, is about being prepared to give Christianity a fresh look, in a new, post-atheist context. If it is true, though, that to say the same thing in a new age you have to say it differently, then Christianity is always having to become 'new'. I have, nevertheless, stressed clear continuities with the past. This is not simply to reassure the traditionalists. It is due to the fact that this is how religions, and human culture, work. The limited (revised Liberal Protestant) strand I have sought to accentuate is my particular preference. I don't think it's the only way. But nor do I think every way is equally plausible or acceptable. I simply think it's a good and fruitful way of trying to kick-start Christianity in Britain. If this particular strand of Christianity can re-find and re-shape itself, and offer itself anew to the range of 'bemused enquirers' who dip in and out of Christianity, or observe it with interest, then it will be of benefit not merely to those who try it. It will be of benefit to Christianity itself, and to British society. That conviction lies at the heart of this book. My hope is that some of its readers might at least put my hunch to the test.

This book started off
(young) vather but the last part I
vaguer. Maybe a 'twentysomething'
should shut up & let the
class get on with it!
So ranging these issues were
(around) long before I (Paul)
was born !
These are many practical
issues not even hinted at.

Notes

Introduction

1. J. Craske and C. Marsh (eds), *Methodism and the Future*, London: Cassell, 1999, p. 5.
2. Interview from 16 January 1995, printed in *Third Way* (March 1995), pp. 12–15, here p. 15.

1. Finding a Place to Start

1. The complex interrelationship of capitalism, opposition to capitalism, war and religion have, of course, taken a new twist since the destruction of the World Trade Center on 11 September 2001.
2. I mean 'relative' here in two senses: relative to the many in their age-group who are not explicitly attached to Christianity in any meaningful, life-shaping way, and relative to the greater number aged fifty and over who remain church-goers.
3. It is possible I'd have studied locally and lived at home, as happens much more now due to the ending of full maintenance grants. But I think it unlikely as 'going to university' and 'moving away from home' were much more synonymous, and arguably, a much more life-changing experience from the 1960s through to the 1980s than can often be true today.
4. I must also record, sadly, that sometimes there is clear evidence of people who 'make it' being very ready to pull the ladder up after them, or in expecting too little intellectually of people from the same social background as they came from.

2. Still Spiritual after All These Years

1. It could be claimed that this is changing since the militantly secular period of the 1970s. But even though governments do now relate more to religious groups, it could still be questioned whether this is

more out of economic or political expediency than wisdom or ideological necessity.

2. For a recent re-assertion of the thesis, see e.g., S. Bruce, *Religion in the Modern World: From Cathedrals to Cults*, Oxford: Oxford University Press, 1996. A vigorous rebuttal can be found in D. Lyon, *Jesus in Disneyland*, Oxford: Polity Press, 2000.

3. Which is to say that this present book cannot present a full, short, systematic Christian theology. The most it can do is show how Christian belief and thought is drawn upon in practice (e.g., via its reference to the person of Jesus Christ, pp. 84–6, to the doctrine of God, pp. 108–9, to salvation, p. 100, to resurrection, p. 85 or to the Church, pp. 104–6 and passim).

4. To cite an obvious example: when claims are made that those who destroyed the World Trade Center acted in the name of Islam, then it is not merely non-Muslims who raise questions.

5. These would, strictly speaking, be resuscitations, not resurrections.

3. Available Resources, Persistent Traditions

1. A. Dulles, *The Catholicity of the Church*, Oxford: Clarendon Press, 1985, p. 185 (reprinted in A. E. McGrath (ed.), *The Christian Theology Reader*, Oxford and Cambridge MA.: Blackwell, 1995, p. 285).

2. It is intriguing that whilst churches often continue to struggle with the way they lift clergy out from amongst the people and seem to make them different, lessons from social-psychology are being learned across many professions about the human need to have embodied representative (even uniformed) figures within groups. It is not, then, such an unusual thing. These are not necessarily 'experts'. Medical doctors need to be; mayors do not. *!*

3. For a compact, if difficult, introduction to lines of thinking in Radical Orthodoxy, see J. Milbank, C. Pickstock and G. Ward (eds), *Radical Orthodoxy*, London and New York: Routledge, 1999.

4. See, e.g., his *Speeches on Religion* on 1799 (latest English translation [of first German edition] ed. R. Crouter, *On Religion: Speeches to Its Cultured Despisers*, Cambridge: Cambridge University Press, 1988), and *The Christian Faith* of 1821–2; 2nd edn 1830; latest English edition, Edinburgh: T&T Clark, 1999). Schleiermacher was in many respects a traditional dogmatician in the Reformed tradition. His main concern was to interpret traditional Christian

theology in a new age. He was interested in Christian mission in so far as he wanted to try and articulate for the benefit of his contemporaries (the religious despisers, or the culturally disinterested) what Christianity had to offer the well-to-do and the learned in late-eighteenth-/early-nineteenth-century Berlin.

5. The manifesto is G. Lindbeck, *The Nature of Doctrine*, London: SPCK, 1984.

6. This point will be developed further in Chapter 5 (in relation to discussion starters 61 and 62).

4. *A Chastened Liberalism*

1. Whether such a new form of Christianity should be called 'liberalism' at all, of course, is a moot point. In offering this proposal I am simply showing how much I learned from some of the creative forms of Christianity I encountered in the 1970s. I use the terms, however, to preserve a continuity with a style of Christianity which currently receives so much undeserved attack. That I am not alone in thinking that this is a fruitful way forward is confirmed, e.g., in J. Jobling and I. Markham (eds), *Theological Liberalism*, London: SPCK, 2000.

2. For a brief attempt to show how liberalisms interweave and an example of how theological liberalism has affected theological education, see my essay 'The Experience of Theological Education: Maintaining a "Liberal" Agenda in a Post-Liberal Age' in M. Chapman (ed.), *The Future of Liberal Theology*, Aldershot and Burlington VT: Ashgate, 2002.

3. The question of what we may call the 'receptivity' of human beings to divine things, and whether such receptivity can be entertained as occurring without fresh, direct divine assistance (revelation) constitutes a major fault line through the whole of Christian thought and practice. It affects differences between Roman Catholics and Protestants, between different kinds of Protestants (e.g., Lutherans and Methodists), and even between different types of evangelical. It takes shape in such questions as whether human beings always retain a sense of their being made in God's image (i.e., God always has a foothold in human life), or whether the image is lost or so tarnished that nothing in the human make-up enables them to perceive or receive God. Clearly, liberalism tends towards a positive view of the human being, and its retention of the divine image to a significant extent.

[handwritten marginal note:] ← Yes — but what A Evolution?

4. The allusion is to 'New Labour's' commitment to a threefold agenda: education, education, and education around the time of the British General Election in 1997.

5. J. Bowden, *Voices in the Wilderness*, London: SCM Press, 1977.

6. J. A. T. Robinson, *Honest to God*, London: SCM Press, 1963 (latest edn 2001).

7. M. Gibbs and T. R. Morton, *God's Frozen People: A book for – and about – ordinary Christians*, London and Glasgow: Fontana, 1964.

8. M. Gibbs and T. R. Morton, *God's Lively People: Christians in Tomorrow's World*, London: Fontana, 1971.

9. It must also be borne in mind that attention to theory, as opposed to practice, does not always free the mind. All theorizing is itself situated, and located within its own sociological and political world. Freedom of the mind, it can now be seen, occurs only when a person is invited to inhabit many, sometimes conflicting, 'communities of practice' within which different approaches to life are operative (see further n.14 below).

10. The illustration is from P. Berger, cited in Stewart Sutherland's article 'Damnation' in A. Richardson and J. Bowden (eds), *A New Dictionary of Christian Theology*, London: SCM Press, 1983, pp. 143–4. Berger uses it as an argument against liberal theology. It only works as such if it is assumed that liberalism assumes that 'anything goes', which is precisely the point I oppose here.

11. This is a clearer example than many that could be cited, of course. But this is the difficult territory into which liberalism has been willing to enter, being accused of over-caution, unwillingness to make commitments, over-dependence on rationality and argument and indifference as a result.

12. Though even then, it is worth asking whether such a belief could ever be totally harmless to those who hold it.

13. For a practical theological critique of Methodist understandings of 'fellowship', see my essay 'A training-ground for forgiveness: Methodism and "fellowship" in Craske and Marsh (eds), *Methodism and the Future*, pp. 100–14.

14. This picks up the insight emphasized by post-liberals, which itself relates to an epistemological shift in Western culture towards situated views of knowledge and learning. Such views emphasize that we are all always located within 'communities of practice' and cannot pretend either that the mind occupies no physical space and exists in disembodied form, or that the individual exists in splendid isolation. The important critique of post-liberalism must be

re-asserted here, however, i.e., that it is prone to make do with religious ghettoes, otherwise religion can be accepted as merely a tribal practice.

15. A. Storr, *Solitude: A Return to the Self*, New York: Ballantine Books, 1988, p. 1.

16. Such a view could be opposed by the work of, e.g., Grace Davie, who (in *Religion in Modern Europe: A Memory Mutates*, Oxford: Oxford University Press, 2000) argues for the existence and significance of 'vicarious memory' and 'vicarious religion' throughout European culture. Whilst accepting the tenor of Davie's argument, the point I am making here concerns belief, and the internalization of values. Without this, it seems to me, the 'vicarious religion' by which Europeans by and large are currently trying to muddle through is at best nostalgia, and at worst a moral and spiritual vacuum.

5. *How to be a Protesting Christian without being Anti-Catholic*

1. Interestingly, though used as a term to denote those supporting religious freedom, in origin it was never a term which indicated totally free choice of religion. Like later discussion of the 1776 declaration of independence of the USA, the argument for freedom of religion was never either an argument for complete individualism, or for irreligion.

2. K. Leech, *The Eye of the Storm*, London: Darton, Longman & Todd, 1992, p. 126. Just a few pages before (p. 123) Leech had been more cautious and less optimistic about the possibilities of Anglo-Catholicism in particular. But his reference to 'the conceptual limitations of Reformation theology, especially . . . its individualism' suggests he would not agree that either liberalism or Protestantism might contribute to the task he correctly identifies as necessary. Helpfully, the anonymous reader for SCM Press of the draft of this book wondered whether the disagreement I explore in this section not only showed that Leech is more liberal Protestant than he would admit, but also that I more liberal Catholic than I am aware!

3. Here are a few: W. Pauck, *The Heritage of the Reformation*, London, Oxford and New York: Oxford University Press, 1950 (enlarged edn 1961), J. Dillenberger and C. Welch, *Protestant Christianity: Interpreted Through Its Development*, New York: Charles Scribner's Sons, 1954, M. Marty, *Protestantism*, London: Weidenfeld & Nicolson, 1972, D. A. Rausch and C. H. Voss,

Protestantism: *Its Modern Meaning*, Philadelphia: Fortress Press, 1987, F. W. Graf and K. Tanner (eds), *Protestantische Identität Heute*, Gütersloh: Gütersloher Verlagshaus Gerd Mohn, 1992.

4. Dillenberger and Welch, *Protestant Christianity*, p. 313–14. The twentieth-century German-American theologian Paul Tillich called this the 'Protestant Principle'. See, e.g., P. Tillich, *The Protestant Era*, Chicago: University of Chicago Press, 1948 (abridged edn, 1957), esp. ch. XI.

5. Mary Norton Kratt, *Southern is . . .*, Atlanta: Peachtree Publishers, 1985.

6. There is therefore no contradiction between 'putting God first' and 'being Christocentric'. Christocentrism is merely the main Christian way of putting God first.

7. Dillenberger and Welch, *Protestant Christianity*, pp. 316–18, 322.

8. I have argued this case in relation to the Methodist presbyterate in 'Priests and Prophets but not Servants: The Presbyterate between the Body of Christ and the Reign of God' in P. Luscombe and E. Shreeve (eds), *What is a Minister?*, Peterborough: Epworth Press, 2002.

9. Bruce, *Religion*, p. 230. I shall deal with the second part of the quotation in Chapter 6.

10. White, Anglo-Saxon Protestants, as discussed on p. 11 above.

11. In Roman Catholicism, such developments have been handled especially in discussions about 'inculturation' and indigenized churches.

12. I first came across the notion of 'somebodiness' in the writings of Martin Luther King Jr. See, e.g., 'The Case Against "Tokenism"' (dating from 1962), reprinted in *A Testament of Hope: The Essential Writings of Martin Luther King Jr*, San Francisco: Harper, 1986, pp. 106–11, esp. p. 108.

13. This is, in any case, a feature of the Christian doctrine of creation.

14. After writing this section I came across Amanda Porterfield's *The Transformation of American Religion: The Story of a Late Twentieth-Century Awakening*, New York: Oxford University Press, 2001. This stimulating, well-written study offers a powerful argument for the value of tracing some seemingly unlikely trajectories through the history of American religion. The persistent, positive influence of Puritanism, and its apparent mutation into other forms of benevolent living, is worth noting. The question remains on both sides of the Atlantic how essential it may prove to be in the longer term to recover or maintain more of the religious dimensions of Puritan thought, belief and practice than our societies seem ready to accept.

15. Though the existence of *The Times* preaching competition and the resurgence of the work of the 'College of Preachers' may offer counter-evidence, as may the emergence of many recent studies of the practice of preaching (especially from the USA). See, e.g., Gerd Theissen, *The Sign Language of Faith: Opportunities for Preaching Today*, London: SCM Press, 1995 and R. J. Allen et al., *Theology for Preaching: Authority, Truth and Knowledge of God in a Postmodern Ethos*, Nashville: Abingdon Press, 1997. *MPH series : shame on you to omitting it !*

16. See, e.g., P .C. Finney (ed.), *Seeing Beyond the Word: Visual Arts and the Calvinist Tradition*, Grand Rapids: Eerdmans, 1999, and also the work of Frank Burch Brown, Colleen McDannell and David Morgan.

17. C. Jones, G. Wainwright and E. Yarnold SJ (eds), *The Study of Spirituality*, London: SPCK, 1986, esp. sections VIII C1–3, and 5–7. For a reader in English spirituality contemporary with the Wesleys, see D. L. Jeffrey, *A Burning and a Shining Light: English Spirituality in the Age of Wesley*, Grand Rapids: Eerdmans, 1987. For a recent collection of texts of Anglican spirituality see G. Rowell et al. (eds), *Love's Redeeming Work*, Oxford: Oxford University Press, 2001. Many of the volumes in the SPCK/Paulist Press 'The Classics of Western Spirituality' series offer texts from British Protestant writers, e.g., William Law, George Herbert, John and Charles Wesley, as well as Protestants from elsewhere: Martin Luther, Johann Arndt, the Pietists. *Gordon Wakefield's contribution—*

18. Though see J. Saxbee, *Liberal Evangelism*, London: SPCK, 1994 and C. Marsh, *Questioning Evangelism: A Contribution from a Liberal Perspective*, Nottingham: Grove Books, 1993.

6. *Contemporary Christianity and the Possibility of Responsible Faith*

1. N. Postman, *Amusing Ourselves to Death: Public Discourse in the Age of Show Business*, London: Methuen, 1987.
2. Bruce, *Religion*, p. 10.
3. It would also be fair to press Bruce to clarify how the proliferation of belief in angels, fairies, crystals, crop circles, and various forms of healing (to name but a few current trends) fits in with the secularization thesis.
4. 'Myth' is, of course, a more helpful word, though it creates other problems for those who equate myth with fiction. But as we now know, truth and reality are not handled only via factual accounts of things.

5. *Times Higher Education Supplement*, 10 August 2001, p. 26. The reference is to Robert D. Putnam's *Bowling Alone: The Collapse and Revival of American Community*, New York: Touchstone, 2000.

6. See most recently on 'cell churches': P. Potter and J. Jones, *The Challenge of Cell Church*, London: Bible Reading Fellowship, 2001.

7. And it must be acknowledged that Methodist historians have frequently uncovered less rosy details of Methodist classes and bands than those perpetuated in Methodist mythology.

8. Most notably, the '9 o'clock Service' (NOS) in Sheffield.

9. I am not aware where this phrase was first used. I have, however, encountered it in the writings of British Methodist ecumenist Geoffrey Wainwright.

10. The parallel between being religious and learning a language has been stressed especially in post-liberalism (see, e.g., George Lindbeck's *The Nature of Doctrine*, London: SPCK, 1984). The parallel is useful, if limited. Pressed too far, it ceases to work, as one cannot perhaps be as fully 'bilingual' in religions as one can be in languages, however intimate a knowledge one might have of another religious tradition.

Appendix 1

'The 95 Theses' (Discussion Starters)

(Chapter 1)

1. No religion or world-view can, or should, dodge questions of biology, embodiment and sexual identity.
2. No religion or world-view can, or should, dodge questions of sexual orientation.
3. Our habits of consumption implicate us daily in a messy and complex world.
4. The fact that the membership of the churches is ageing and declining substantially does not mean that Christianity has nothing to offer the under-fifties.
5. Where you've lived is who you are.
6. Ethnicity matters.
7. Religious particularity matters. Denominations may be less important than they were, but respect for them is necessary. Otherwise, we're too general and universal for our own good.
8. Family histories interweave with the development of our beliefs and values to a profound extent, and are often insufficiently examined.
9. Parenthood can be preoccupying.
10. Meaningful activity (work) is crucial in human life, but is not everything.
11. The psychological aspects of the question of 'class and Christianity' in Britain have been inadequately explored.
12. All religion is political.

(Chapter 2)

13. Western society has undoubtedly become more 'secular' over the past couple of centuries.

14. There are different kinds of western 'secularization'.
15. Britain is less secular than often appears.
16. British people are often more secular than they realize.
17. World-views and value-systems are rarely recognized and shared.
18. British culture suffers from a legacy of bad religion.
19. We live in a 'post-atheist' age.
20. Spirituality and religion are not the same thing.
21. There is a 'spirituality boom' happening at present, to which there are both positive and negative aspects.
22. Mainstream religions need to re-assert themselves.
23. Christianity has to re-define and re-present itself in twenty-first-century Britain.
24. The place of a religion (e.g., Christianity) in a person's life in twenty-first-century Britain has to be made more plausible.
25. There can be no dodging of the question of whether there is an 'absolute religion'.
26. We don't have the grounds to conclude what an 'absolute religion' might be.
27. Concluding that we don't know what an 'absolute religion' might look like does not validate 'pick-and-mix' spirituality, or imply that participation in a religion is a matter of indifference.
28. The rediscovery of religion is a global phenomenon.
29. The rediscovery of religion has its dangers.
30. Much of the new energy in Christianity as a world religion comes from outside the (North) West.

(Chapter 3)

31. We all stand within an assortment of 'traditions', because if we didn't, we wouldn't be human.
32. It is crucial to know which traditions you stand in.
33. From the catholic tradition we learn the importance of church order and of liturgy.
34. From Radical Orthodoxy we learn of the contemporary importance of liturgy, in the context of a trenchant critique of modernity's influence upon Christianity.
35. Liberalism shows how it is possible to remain a religious believer within the post-Enlightenment world.
36. Post-liberalism re-asserts the corporate nature of Christianity,

the crucial role of the Church and the importance of narrative in Christian belief and practice.

37. The charismatic and pentecostal movements keep alive in Christianity the dangerous memory of the workings of the spirit of God throughout the world.

38. Evangelicalism emphasizes personal faith, Jesus-centredness and the sovereign action of God.

39. Liberation theologies have contributed to the questioning of privatized, individualistic forms of Christianity, and have challenged Christians to look at the social and material aspects of Christian faith in God.

40. Denominations are far from dead and are likely to continue in some form. But the primary Christian groupings in the future may be theological movements and spiritual traditions.

41. Christians working with other Christians (ecumenism) is the only way forward. But ecumenism will not mean uniformity. It will mean unity in diversity.

(Chapter 4)

42. Christianity in the West is in danger of becoming totally ghetto-ized.

43. We need a 'new Christian liberalism'.

44. The new Christian liberalism will creatively interact with non-Christian thought forms.

45. The new Christian liberalism accepts the critique of liberalism's past tendency to promote individualism.

46. The new Christian liberalism will draw more on Christianity's public role.

47. The new Christian liberalism will build on its known, past commitment to theological education and critical thinking. In so doing, it will again risk the charge of élitism.

48. The new Christian liberalism will resist being allied with an 'anything goes' culture.

49. New forms of Christianity must be unreservedly 'secular'.

50. Secular encounters with God need religious communities to be known as such.

51. There is no such thing as Christianity for solitary believers.

52. The notion of a 'networked' and 'networking' understanding of the Church has considerable value.

53. 'Virtual communities' are not enough.
54. Religious believers remain individual human beings, however important the emphases upon the social dimensions of religious belief undoubtedly are.

(Chapter 5)

55. Protestantism is not a denomination.
56. We need not all be Protestants now, but a form of post-modern Protestantism would be a welcome development in British Christianity.
57. Some of the best Protestants are Roman Catholics.
58. Protestantism seeks to put God first.
59. Protestantism is unreservedly critical.
60. Protestantism feeds the independent spirit.
61. Protestantism is Christocentric.
62. Christocentrism does not simply mean 'putting Jesus first'.
63. Protesting Christians can be lay or ordained.
64. Protestantism promotes individuality and freedom, but remains committed to the creation of Christian community and a civil society.
65. Protestantism is attractive to protestors.
66. Protestantism should especially appeal to oppressed groups.
67. Protestantism incorporates a theology of 'somebodiness'.
68. Protestantism's crucial contemporary protest must be against consumerism.
69. It is time to develop a 'New Puritanism'.
70. Protestantism tends to produce wordy thinkers rather than pray-ers, but there is a rich vein of types of Protestant spirituality to be drawn on.
71. The emphasis on words in Protestantism relates to the stimulus of thought, as well as belief and practice.
72. Different types of Christianity will appeal to different psychological types.
73. Liberal Protestants need not be tentative about trying to persuade others to become Christians.

(*Chapter 6*)

74. In an age when we're in danger of 'amusing ourselves to death', we must ensure that we keep in touch with things that matter most.
75. Religion is therapy for those of us who can't, or don't want to, afford expensive therapists.
76. It is a mistake to build a viable form of contemporary religion on supernaturalism.
77. It is equally a mistake to build a viable form of religion on the assumption that religion is a wholly human creation.
78. Churches do not have, and never have had, a monopoly on truth, even though the 'Christendom model' of Christianity has been able to operate as if this were the case. Lots of different bodies and movements will help us work out what to think and believe, and how to behave.
79. In a fragmented, yet tradition-saturated, age, it is vital to make choices about particular world-views, communities and groups which it is worth attaching oneself to.
80. 'Attachment' to a world-view, community or group means being able to specify a particular form of loyal commitment, otherwise it means little.
81. Commitment to Christianity will entail making specific commitment to particular forms and understandings of Christianity.
82. There will have to be new forms of 'church'.
83. Worship will take new forms, and will often not take place on Sundays.
84. 'Commitment to Christianity' may mean many things.
85. 'Commitment to God' can mean many things.
86. The 'agnostic onlookers' and 'theological non-realists' must not be excluded from the Christian search for God.
87. We must accept that religions are in the business of trying to identify and articulate something more than is given an account of by sociologists of religion.
88. Christians will need a portable faith capable of being expressed and enriched much more flexibly than most current models of Christian thought and practice will find comfortable.
89. The traditions and groups to which Christians are attached and committed will need to challenge, as well as support and enrich, Christians, otherwise individual Christians could simply control the content of their faith, and their understanding of God.

90. Within an understanding of church as a 'network of networks' Christianity can in future be a network of groups, formal and informal, of varying styles of Christianity.

91. The involvement in 'the Christian community' of an individual Christian (in whatever form and at whatever point the individual exercises that contact) must lead to creative theological interpretation of that individual's participation in other relationships and communities.

92. Religions will need to take their educative role more seriously, not simply in terms of 'grooming people in the faith', but in making their own contribution to people's understanding of how important religion is in British society.

93. Local forms of religion (e.g., Christian churches) need to be contexts in which people have doors opened up to the wider world. *[handwritten: Just they will have gone!]*

94. Through their involvement in religion locally, people will be encouraged to reflect on, as well as participate in, the things that matter locally.

95. Christianity will only reveal itself to be a viable form of religion in contemporary Britain if it begins to work again for people as a source of personal, social and political transformation.

[handwritten: What does it try to do. how?]

Appendix 2

Using This Book Individually and in Small Groups

This book has been structured in such a way that it can function as a thought-provoker both for individuals and for groups.

Individuals could read one of the discussion starters ('theses') each day over a period of just over three months. Though the discussion starters are of unequal length, and vary in the extent to which they remain abstract points, or use illustrative material, they each focus on something distinct. Those who scribble in margins of books should therefore be encouraged to take up their pencils and get to work each day in response to the topics raised. Or those who write diaries or journals should incorporate their reflections on the daily themes in the entries they write. Alternatively, readers could keep a notebook specifically devoted to the material which the book introduces, and the questions it raises. Here are some of the questions you could ask yourself each day:

- Do I agree with this? Why/Why not?
- What evidence am I bringing to mind to agree/disagree?
- In what way/s am I challenged by today's discussion topic?
- What aspects of my own life/experience/thought/belief are being touched on today?
- In what way/s am I being expected to re-think what I think/believe?
- What new insights/thoughts come to me as a result of today's reading and reflection?
- What else do I need to do/read/think about to get clearer about the topic raised?
- Who should I speak with about today's reading?

Individuals who use the book in the above way could, of course, after a while also form groups.

The book could also be used by groups from the start.

Small Groups would probably need to be already established (e.g., as study, house, reflection, fellowship groups) to get the most from the book – at least, to handle it sequentially – Chapter 1 would be a tough place to start for a group newly formed. Established groups would have a ready-made six-session programme available, with the following structure:

- Who are we?
- What's our context?
- Where is Christian theology up to?
- What can Christian liberalism offer us?
- What does it mean to be Protestant?
- What sort of Christian can one be today?

One way of handling the material would be for everyone to get their own copy of the book and read through the relevant chapter before each session. Either a group leader, or an appointed person in the group, could then be responsible each time for introducing the discussion on the assumption that all have looked through the material. In each session the focus could be on:

- the main thrust of the chapter (and whether the group thinks it right or wrong);
- the particular points that group members found most significant or telling;
- how the material from the chapter does/does not connect with the concrete life experience or context of the group itself;
- where the group thinks the chapter's material is heading in relation to the actual future shape of Christianity in Britain.

Alternatively, using Appendix 1, the discussion starters alone could be made available before each session. One member of the group could then have the responsibility to summarize the main points of the chapter. That same person, or a different person, could then use one or more of the discussion starters as a main 'jumping-off point' for the discussion, accepting that it is less likely, if all do not have the whole book before them, that the group would remain focused on the overall thrust of the chapter as a whole.

For new groups formed in order to discuss the book, it may be best for Chapter 1 to be visited at the end of the exercise. Though it would be important for readers to work through Chapter 1 to begin with for themselves, and write notes on their own response to that material in the form of a summary of the key influences upon them, it might not be wise, unless a leader felt especially confident to do so, to begin a group's programme at that point. But I'd be pleased if I am proved quite wrong!

Appendix 3

For Further Exploration

Readers who want to take matters further, beyond this book, could go in all sorts of directions. The most important thing of all would be to attach yourself to others (Christian or not) who are exploring in a similar way to you, and who want to wrestle with the issues that the book raises. If you do want to take matters in a specifically Christian direction, then you'd be best to link up with a Christian group of some kind. If it's further reading you're after, then in addition to books mentioned in the footnotes to the chapters, you could look at the following.

On Christianity and the Religious Scene in Britain Today

Grace Davie, *Religion in Britain since 1945* (Oxford: Blackwell, 1994) presents the case for 'believing without belonging', arguing that there's more belief around than we might think, even if people don't join religious groups as much as they used to. She thus opposes the so-called 'secularization thesis'. Callum Brown, *The Death of Christian Britain* (London and New York: Routledge, 2001) offers a historical account (covering 1800–2000) in support of the 'secularization thesis'. Steve Bruce, *Religion in the Modern World* (Oxford: Oxford University Press, 1996) follows a similar line, not simply dealing with Britain. Bruce's *Religion in Modern Britain* (Oxford: Oxford University Press, 1995) is a useful account of the state of religions in Britain. Philip Richter and Leslie Francis, *Gone But Not Forgotten* (London: Darton, Longman & Todd, 1998) is a study of why people leave churches, with proposals for what might help leavers to return. It's a sobering account of some of the main reasons why churches in Britain have become so numerically weak. Those wanting to dip their toe into recent British (or at least English) church history could do a lot worse than start with

He rejects the secularization thesis and invents his own !! - based on feminism.

No! It is quite different. It is the familiar secularization thesis

Adrian Hastings' excellent *A History of English Christianity 1920–2000* (London: SCM Press, 2001). Studies of Christianity and the religious scene which go beyond Britain, yet which are both interesting and pertinent, include David Lyon, *Jesus in Disneyland: Religion in Postmodern Times* (Oxford: Polity Press, 2000), Robert Wuthnow, *Christianity in the Twenty-first Century* (New York and Oxford: Oxford University Press, 1993), the classic sociological study of American society by Robert Bellah and others, *Habits of the Heart* (2nd edn; Berkeley, Los Angeles and London: University of California Press, 1996) and Amanda Porterfield's recent account of developments in American religion, *The Transformation of American Religion: The Story of a Late Twentieth-Century Awakening* (New York: Oxford University Press, 2001).

On Christianity's History

Useful introductory, but substantial, studies of Christianity in both a historical and a world context include John McManners (ed.), *The Oxford History of Christianity* (Oxford and New York: Oxford University Press, 1993) and Adrian Hastings (ed.), *A World History of Christianity* (London: Cassell, 1999).

On Basic Themes in Christian Theology

Without doubt the best single volume introducing Christian theology today is the best-selling text book by Alister McGrath, *Christian Theology: An Introduction* (3rd edn; Oxford: Blackwell, 2001). Publisher and author together have sought to develop the book substantially through each edition, so that its inevitable biases are not too off-putting. It succeeds well as a source of information and a stimulus for further study and reflection, containing useful bibliographies to enable more extensive enquiry. For imaginative ways of trying to work through Christian themes in full awareness of the context of world faiths, see, e.g., N. Smart and S. Konstantine, *Christian Systematic Theology in a World-Context* (London: Marshall Pickering, 1991) and the recent writings of Keith Ward, e.g., *Religion and Revelation* (Oxford: Oxford University Press, 1994), *Religion and Creation* (Oxford: Oxford University Press, 1996), *Religion and Human Nature* (Oxford: Oxford University

Press, 1998), *Religion and Community* (Oxford: Oxford University Press, 2000) and, in succinct form, *Christianity: A Short Introduction* (Oxford: Oneworld, 2000). ✓

✓ *God.* (Oxworld 2002.)

On Movements, Styles of Theology and Key Christian Thinkers

Chapter 3 of this book draws on many different movements, and most used receive a section in Chapter 4 of McGrath's *Christian Theology: An Introduction.* There are, though, many separate books on particular movements. Here are just a few: D. L. Edwards and J. Stott, *Essentials: A liberal-evangelical dialogue* (London: Hodder & Stoughton, 1988); B. M. G. Reardon, *Liberal Protestantism* (London: A & C Black, 1968); Walter Hollenweger, *The Pentecostals* (London: SCM Press, 1972); D. Tidball, *Who Are the Evangelicals?* (London: Marshall Pickering, 1994); A. E. McGrath, *Evangelicalism and the Future of Christianity* (rev. edn, Downers Grove: InterVarsity Press, 1995); C. Boff and L. Boff, *Introducing Liberation Theology* (London: Burns & Oates, 1987); P. Berryman, *Liberation Theology* (London: Tauris, 1987); C. Rowland (ed.), *The Cambridge Companion to Liberation Theology* (Cambridge: Cambridge University Press, 1999); J. Atherton (ed.), *Social Christianity: A Reader* (London: SPCK, 1994). Much of the writing on post-liberalism and Radical Orthodoxy is difficult stuff. Two substantial (but not easy) textbooks which incorporate writings from these movements are: J. Webster and George P. Schner (eds), *Theology after Liberalism: A Reader* (Oxford: Blackwell, 2000) and G. Ward (ed.), *The Postmodern God: A Reader* (Oxford: Blackwell, 1997). Don Cupitt, *Taking Leave of God* (London: SCM Press, 1980) is the manifesto of 'theological non-realism' and Colin Crowder (ed.), *God and Reality* (London: Mowbray, 1997) offers essays discussing this option. A. E. McGrath (ed.), *The Blackwell Encyclopaedia of Modern Christian Thought* (Oxford: Blackwell, 1993) contains many useful essays on modern movements and thinkers. Trevor Hart (ed.), *The Dictionary of Historical Theology* (Carlisle: Paternoster Press; Grand Rapids: Eerdmans, 2000) covers the whole of Christian history, as does Adrian Hastings (ed.), *The Oxford Companion to Christian Thought* (Oxford: Oxford University Press, 2000). David Ford (ed.), *The Modern Theologians* (Oxford: Blackwell, 1997) is a giant of a book with a range of essays of varying levels of difficulty on modern theologians and movements. It's a great collection but isn't a book for beginners. For those who find large textbooks intimidating, and dictionaries and encyclopaedias off-putting, Colin Blakely's handy, and at times amusing, introduction to some major figures in Christian history, *Great Christian Thinkers: A Starter Kit* (London: SPCK, 2000) will be ideal. Readers who want to tease out more about the Reformation and the origins of Protestantism could turn to Carter Lindberg, *The European Reformations* (Oxford: Blackwell, 1996) and Steven ✓ Ozment, *Protestants: The Birth of a Revolution* (New York: Doubleday, 1992; London: Fontana Press, 1993).

On the Bible

Short, introductory guides to the Bible for those who feel overawed by its texts should find John Barton, *Making the Christian Bible* (London: Darton, Longman & Todd, 1997), or his *What is the Bible?* (rev. edn, London: SPCK, 1997) or John Riches, *The Bible: A Very Short Introduction* (Oxford: Oxford University Press, 2000) helpful. John Rogerson has written *An Introduction to the Bible* (Harmondsworth: Penguin, 1999) and edited *The Oxford Illustrated History of the Bible* (Oxford: Oxford University Press, 2001), for those who want to be stretched a bit further. More demanding still are histories of recent interpretation of the Bible. Historical studies which also address issues raised by the task of biblical interpretation include *The Interpretation of the New Testament 1861–1986* by Stephen Neill and Tom Wright (Oxford and New York: Oxford University Press, 1988) and *Biblical Interpretation* by Robert Morgan with John Barton (Oxford and New York: Oxford University Press, 1988). Various series of books look in more detail at different parts of the Bible. The Cassell/Continuum Biblical Studies Series is especially handy. For starters, see, e.g., Clive Marsh and Steve Moyise, *Jesus and the Gospels: An Introduction* (London: Cassell, 1999) and David Horrell, *An Introduction to the Study of Paul* (London: Continuum, 2001).

For Readings from Christian History

A number of 'Readers' are available for those who want to read key thinkers of Christian history in their own words. The companion volume to Alister McGrath's introduction to Christian theology is *The Christian Theology Reader* (2ⁿᵈ edn; Oxford: Blackwell, 2001). Hugh Kerr (ed.), *Readings in Christian Thought* (Nashville: Abingdon Press, 1990) and Peter C. Hodgson and Robert H. King (eds), *Readings in Christian Theology* (Philadelphia: Fortress Press, 1985) offer two further selections, the latter offering long extracts. Ann Loades (ed.), *Feminist Theology: A Reader* (London: SPCK, 1990) provides a selection of women writers from Christian history.

On Spirituality (Christian and Beyond)

A good place to start would be Alister McGrath's introduction *Christian Spirituality* (Oxford: Blackwell, 1999). For those who want to dig much deeper, SCM Press and Crossroad have been publishing a large series of books of essays called 'World Spirituality'. Three volumes (nos. 16 to 18 in the series) are entitled *Christian Spirituality* (edited by B. McGinn and J. Meyendorff, Jill Raitt, and L. Dupré and D. E. Saliers respectively). From the rest in the series, of particular relevance to this present book is Peter H. Van Ness, *Spirituality and the Secular Quest* (London: SCM Press; New York: Crossroad, 1996). An example of a single volume introduction to seven mainstream religions (Hinduism, Buddhism, Confucianism, Taoism, Judaism, Christianity and Islam), written by participants in those religions, is Arvind Sharma (ed.), *Our Religions* (New York: Harper Collins, 1993). A study which helps in the understanding of how spirituality has developed in very concrete terms in the West in the past fifty years, using the USA as an example, is Robert Wuthnow, *After Heaven* (Berkeley, Los Angeles and London: University of California Press, 1998). A highly practical, and underrated, book which explores the possibility of people coming to Christian faith in a British context is *The Search for Faith and the Witness of the Church* (London: Church House Publishing, 1996). Unlike other books recommended throughout this Appendix, this is a church report. This will put off some readers, but its format may be helpful for those whose jobs usually require them to read texts of a similar style.

Christianity and the www

McGrath's *Christian Theology: An Introduction* contains an appendix listing 'Theological Resources on the Internet'. A fuller directory of sites can be found in V. Blackmore, *God on the Net Year 2002 Edition* (London: Bibles/Liturgical/Music, 2001).

McGrath is
I fear rather
overrated.
When this first came out
a Th(?) Year student at
[Man univ found] 2
fairly bad) mistakes in 2
minutes! No doubt
these were corrected!
Historical Theology
an Introduction —
Blackwell 1998
is another here.
McGrath ok again
ok!

Index